D0874088

ANNEXE DE LA BIBLIOTHÈQUE

uOttawa

LIBRARY ANNEX

SOCIALISTS AND THE BALLOT BOX

mo.

SOCIALISTS AND THE BALLOT BOX
A Historical Analysis

Eric Thomas Chester

BIBLIOTHÈQUES

LIBRARIES

University of

Library of Congress Cataloging in Publication Data

Chester, Eric Thomas.
  Socialists and the ballot box.

  Bibliography: p.
  Includes index.

  1. Socialist—United States—Political activity—History. 2. Socialist parties—United States—History. 3. Political parties—United States—History. 4. Politics, Practical—History. I. Title.
HX89.C49   1985   324.273'7   85-6475
  ISBN 0-03-004142-2 (alk. paper)

HX
89
.C49
1985

Published in 1985 by Praeger Publishers
CBS Educational and Professional Publishing, a Division of CBS Inc.
521 Fifth Avenue, New York, NY 10175 USA

© 1985 Eric Thomas Chester

All rights reserved

56789 052 987654321

Printed in the United States of America on acid-free paper

INTERNATIONAL OFFICES

Orders from outside the United States should be sent to the appropriate address listed below. Orders from areas not listed below should be placed through CBS International Publishing, 383 Madison Ave., New York, NY 10175 USA

Australia, New Zealand
Holt Saunders, Pty. Ltd., 9 Waltham St., Artarmon, N.S.W. 2064, Sydney, Australia

Canada
Holt, Rinehart & Winston of Canada, 55 Horner Ave., Toronto, Ontario, Canada M8Z 4X6

Europe, the Middle East, & Africa
Holt Saunders, Ltd., 1 St. Anne's Road, Eastbourne, East Sussex, England BN21 3UN

Japan
Holt Saunders, Ltd., Ichibancho Central Building, 22-1 Ichibancho, 3rd Floor, Chiyodaku, Tokyo, Japan

Hong Kong, Southeast Asia
Holt Saunders Asia Ltd., 10 Fl, Intercontinental Plaza, 94 Granville Road, Tsim Sha Tsui East, Kowloon, Hong Kong

Manuscript submissions should be sent to the Editorial Director, Praeger Publishers, 521 Fifth Avenue, New York, NY 10175 USA

To my parents

PREFACE

As someone who has been active in socialist politics for more than 20 years, I have participated in several heated debates over issues concerning electoral politics. In each instance, the debate centered on whether and to what extent it was appropriate for socialists to work for candidates running within the Democratic party. Each time those whom I debated were convinced that their support for a specific Democratic candidate represented a strictly tactical response to the exceptional circumstances of that particular election. They further insisted that they remained critical of both of the establishment parties and, in general, that they were still revolutionaries who believed in grass-roots militancy as the only path toward a socialist transformation. Despite these protestations, in each case the decision to back certain liberal Democrats soon led to a fundamental shift in strategic perspective. Indeed, each of these sets of socialists became fervent advocates of strengthening the broad liberal coalition within the Democratic party, and they proceeded to chastise those of us who presented alternative strategies for being ultra-leftist sectarians.

This series of similar experiences piqued my interest. I was eager to place these current debates into historical perspective. Beginning with Marx and Engels, I would examine the socialist tradition, with its commitment to the formation of an independent working class party. I would then trace the evolution of socialist organizations in the United States that had decided to abandon this tradition in order to organize within the Democratic party. My focus would be on exploring how this decision, each time defended initially as tactical and conjunctural, was associated with a profound revision in fundamental world-view and in political practice. I resolved to take as case studies socialist organizations with which I was not directly involved so that I could more objectively examine the trajectory followed by each of these formations. I wound up studying the Communist party of the 1930s and the Shachtman tendency, an offshoot of orthodox Trotskyism.

The hardest part of the project has been limiting its scope. Each topic I have researched has led me to new questions and concerns. Nevertheless, the focal point of the project remains as first conceived. Hopefully, this study will help provide the basis for a more intelligent discussion of this vital issue within the socialist movement.

ACKNOWLEDGMENTS

Many people have contributed to bringing this project to fruition. Julia Wrigley has been of tremendous assistance at every stage with her support, advice, and editorial comments. Carolyn Magid encouraged me to keep going even during the down periods. Two socialists from an earlier generation were of considerable help, my father Harry Chester and Frank Marquart, who has since passed away. Several people read parts of the manuscript and gave me valuable feedback. They include Nancy Wechsler, Peter Drucker, Nelson Lichtenstein, David Finkel, and George Breitman. My editor at Praeger, Lynda Sharp, has made the final stages of the publication process a great deal easier and smoother than I had expected.

Finally, I would like to acknowledge that parts of this work have been previously published in *Changes* and *Against the Current*.

CONTENTS

LIST OF TABLES

SOCIALISTS AND THE BALLOT BOX

1

TWO CONFLICTING WORLD VIEWS

Should socialists work closely with liberals within the Democratic party or should they remain outside of the two-party system in order to be consistent proponents of a new, independent radical party? The issue has been a highly divisive one within the socialist movement, for electoral politics has always been a touchstone on the Left. Indeed this is hardly surprising, since disagreements over electoral politics reflect fundamental differences on the appropriate strategy to be followed in moving toward a socialist society. The core of this underlying division can be characterized as the conflict between reformism and revolutionary socialism.

Of course, the entire spectrum of positions within the Left cannot be reduced to these two conflicting perspectives. Nevertheless, the ongoing debate concerning participation in the Democratic party is closely linked to the fundamental divergence in world views.

A clear understanding of the conflicts over participating within the Democratic party can only be gained when the two contrasting world-views are fully comprehended and when the links between these underlying perspectives and the differing stances toward the Democratic party are established. This introductory section sets this ideological context.

REFORMIST SOCIALISM

Reformists envision the transition to socialism as occurring through the implementation of a continuing series of incremental reforms. These reforms will necessitate a steady expansion of the state's role in the economy. Although reformists stress the importance of electoral victories, they also recognize that ruling class resistance can only be overcome by the concerted and organized pressure of working people. A broad coalition of progressive forces needs to be brought together around a unified set of basic demands.

Nevertheless, reformist socialists have always been extremely sensitive to the potential dangers arising from grass-roots activism. Spontaneous actions generate new demands, demands that could trigger support for repressive measures from elements of the existing power structure. Reformists fear that escalating the militancy of struggle will only lead to increasingly bitter struggles and the possibility of an all-out confrontation.

Thus the pressure exerted by working people on the state must be channeled through bureaucratized institutions and, in particular, through the union structure. Indeed, only the trade unions can provide the organizational base and the financial resources required to sustain a progressive coalition as an effective force in national politics.

Obviously, electoral politics plays a crucial role within the reformist perspective, since it is only on the legislative terrain that one can hope to win incremental gains along a broad front of social issues. For reformists, the critical task for the Left in the current period is to develop and strengthen the progressive coalition within the Democratic party. In this way, it is hoped, the Democratic party can be transformed into a party that consistently defends the interests of working people. Once this is accomplished, the U.S. two-party system can be "realigned" to approach more closely the political systems of Western European countries. The most important organized expression of reformist socialist politics in the United States, the Democratic Socialists of America (DSA), has been outspoken in its pursuit of a realignment strategy.

In one sense, the reformist socialist commitment to working within the Democratic party is unexpected, since those who advocate such a strategy are often ardent admirers of the social democratic parties of Western Europe. These working class parties were initiated by socialists as a direct challenge to the continued allegiance of the working class to the more liberal capitalist parties.

Most reformists within this country would agree in theory with the desirability of an independent working class party, but they also argue that the specific features of the U.S. electoral system act to preclude such a development and to reinforce the two-party system. I believe, on the contrary, that the participation of reformists in the Democratic party reflects their basic perspective and not the exigencies of the U.S. political structure.

If one assumes that only marginal gains can be won and those only through leadership coalitions, then it makes perfect sense to remain within the Democratic party. Certainly if the existing parameters of political discourse are taken as setting the outer boundaries of credible alternatives, then the liberal wing of the Democratic party provides the best hope for working people.

Of course, socialists who pursue a realignment strategy frequently present a set of demands that goes beyond those accepted by mainstream liberal politicians. Indeed, socialists within this tendency see their essential and distinctive role in the progressive coalition as formulating a more coherent and thoroughgoing agenda for structural change. Nevertheless, reformists believe that the securing of fundamental change does not require a sharp break with the existing system and, in particular, with two-party politics. For reformists, there is a smooth linkage between current struggles for immediate demands and the transition to a socialist society. Moreover, realignment politics is not only reformist in the traditional sense that it projects a gradual, electoral transition to a socialist society, but also in the even more restricted sense that it denies the qualitative difference between liberal and radical programs of social change, thereby undercutting the need to directly confront the hold of the Democratic party.

REVOLUTIONARY SOCIALISM

Revolutionary socialists start with the necessity of working toward a definitive break with the existing social system. Capitalism cannot be gradually transformed, but rather a new society can only be created by directly challenging the concentrated power of the governing elite and the corporate rulers. This does not imply that every reform movement is doomed to failure. On the contrary, significant gains can sometimes be won, but only when working people are prepared to exert pressure on the powerful through militant organization and direct action. Furthermore, the dynamics of the system set strictly defined limits on reform movements. Demands that confront capitalist control over key economic and financial resources are met with open resistance, first in the form of a massive outflow of capital to other countries, and ultimately in the form of military violence.

For revolutionary socialists, the primary task of the current period is not the strengthening of the liberal coalition but, instead, the development of a network of movement activists of working people and the oppressed within key organizations. Revolutionaries emphasize the importance of direct action and militant struggles in the deepening of class consciousness.

From such a perspective comes a very different stance toward the trade union leadership, including its more progressive wing. The institutional pressures to conformity increase enormously within the higher ranks of the bureaucracy. To those at the top, stability is paramount. The smooth functioning of the organization is of the utmost concern, even more important than the immediate welfare of the workers or even of the union itself.

The significance of this point has been painfully reinforced by the pattern set over the last few years, as corporation after corporation has confronted entrenched unions with demands for drastic cuts in wages and compromises in working conditions. Defeating these corporate attacks would have required a mobilization of the ranks, with the risk of bitter battles and state repression. An aroused, active membership is a politically aware membership, and an aware membership is likely to limit the perquisites and power of a bureaucratic leadership. Faced with these conflicting pressures, union officials have quietly accepted a long series of major defeats.

The same pattern of bureaucratic entrenchment and a consequent timidity of tactics has been characteristic of the mainstream feminist groups, as well as the leading organizations of the black and Hispanic communities. Thus revolutionaries and reformists have diametrically different attitudes toward the leadership elite of the progressive coalition. Instead of seeing the possibility for fundamental change as dependent on the strengthening of the coalition, revolutionary socialists stress the necessity of breaking with the cautious conservatism of the current leadership through a radicalized movement of grass-roots activists.

THE ELECTORAL ARENA

From a revolutionary socialist perspective, electoral politics has inherent drawbacks that can only be overcome if they are directly addressed and counteracted.

Elections are necessarily passive, particularly when the system of voting reinforces the representative character of the capitalist state. Infrequent elections for candidates whose programs are little known and understood can only act as another object lesson to most working people that their role is to take orders, while an elite makes the key decisions. Participation in elections also reinforces constitutional illusions. No matter what a socialist candidate may say, voters can only understand the existence of a socialist candidacy itself to mean that basic change, and perhaps even the transition to a socialist society, can be attained through electoral victories for socialist candidates.

Despite the intrinsic limitations, electoral politics can provide an important arena in which to deepen class consciousness but only once the working class has formed its own, independent political party. Electoral activity within the framework of a capitalist party can only act to reinforce conflicts among working people, as each group attempts to promote its own narrow interests, even to the harm of the legitimate interests of other oppressed groups. An independent party is a prerequisite for an awareness of the need to struggle around a program that can unite the class as a whole.

Yet a viable radical party can only become a reality after a sustained period of intense political activity leads to the forging of a network of community and shop-floor activists. Only such a network can generate the momentum required for a decisive break with the two-party system. In contrast, a strategy that relies on the progressive union leadership to initiate such a break is bound to fail. The formation of the Cooperative Commonwealth Federation (CCF) in Canada during the years of the Great Depression stands as a pertinent case study.

In 1933, representatives of farmers' cooperatives, socialist groups, and local labor parties met in Regina, Saskatchewan to launch a new party aiming "to replace the present capitalist system . . . by a social order from which the domination and exploitation of one class by another will be eliminated." From the start, the CCF was a major electoral force in western Canada, winning 34 percent of the vote in British Columbia for the 1935 federal elections.[1]

Although the CCF provided an effective framework for a coalition of grass-roots organizations to present a radical alternative to the mainstream politics of the Liberals and Progressive Conservatives, the trade union apparatus continued to back candidates from the two established parties. The CCF repeatedly sought trade union affiliations, but party leaders were met with an almost total rebuff. Activists from the CCF helped to organize the workers of Canada's basic industries into CIO (Congress of Industrial Organizations) unions during the late 1930s, and many of the newly formed CIO unions proceeded to hire CCF supporters for staff positions. Despite these unofficial links, the CIO and its Canadian affiliate, the Canadian Congress of Labour, withheld endorsement of the CCF slate in federal elections until 1943, a decade after the party's formation.[2] Officials of CIO unions were concerned that open support for the CCF would lead the federal government to favor rival unions from the Trades and Labour Congress, the Canadian equivalent of the American Federation of Labor (AFL). One historian of the CCF has concluded that trade union leaders, even the most progressive, "played an inconsequential role in the early affairs of the CCF."[3]

Instead of relying on initiatives from trade union leaders or liberal politicians, socialists should be furthering close ties between militant activists throughout the array of social movements. These links can provide the basis for launching a radical independent party built from below with the active participation of its members. Through this process, hierarchical patterns can be confronted and innovative methods of decision making can be developed to limit the power of those in leadership positions. The new party would thus present a prefigurative expression of the socialist future through its own internal functioning.

Such a grass-roots party will also be much more likely to maintain close ties with activist movements, so that the gap between electoral politics and direct action can be effectively bridged. The Green party of West Germany is an important example of a party that has forged solid links between those active in a variety of social movements and radical politics in the electoral arena.

The Greens originally arose out of the environmental movement, when one organization within this movement decided to field its own candidates in the 1978 provincial elections. In early 1979, organizers from this group approached an umbrella coalition of environmental and antimilitarist organizations for support in running a full slate of candidates for elections to the European parliament. When the Greens gained 900,000 votes in the 1979 elections, the Greens became a highly visible presence in West German politics. Nonsectarian leftists flocked into the new formation, broadening its political perspective and enabling it to reach out to a wider segment of society. The vitality of the Greens was conclusively demonstrated in the federal elections of March 1983, when the party surpassed the 5 percent threshold and thus won representation in the West German parliament, the Bundestag.[4]

By organizing from below, the Green party has placed a premium on the democratic participation of its members. At the base of the party are local chapters that mandate delegates to state and national congresses where basic policy guidelines are determined. These guidelines set policy directions for all Green spokespeople, even those elected to the Bundestag. Furthermore, the Greens have insisted on the rotation of all leaders, so that the party remains truly open to grass-roots initiatives.[5]

The formation of a party similar to the Greens in the United States would dramatically widen the spectrum of legitimate discourse. As in West Germany, the United States has seen the growth of environmental organizations and the antimilitarist movement, as well as the fragmentation and demoralization of the organized Left. For radicals in this country, the Greens provide a successful model for bringing together these varied forces into an independent electoral party that can present a credible alternative to the dominant politics.

Of course, the launching of such a broadly based party would be the basis for a whole new set of problems, reflecting a more advanced political situation. As the party became increasingly successful, pressures would be bound to mount on it to dilute its program in order to widen its electoral base. Furthermore, more moderate elements, who were initially unwilling to join a new party, would be attracted to it as it gained in success. Finally, any institution has the tendency to become rigid and bureaucratic, especially in periods of relative quiescence.

Indeed, during their brief history, the West German Greens have had to confront all of these problems. A mass party is bound to cover a wide spectrum of views, so the existence of a multiplicity of organized tendencies should be seen as the norm. Socialists have coalesced with the Greens to emphasize a more working-class perspective, in distinction to the purely environmental concerns of some Greens. Should a comparable party be formed here, revolutionary socialists would initiate one of several tendencies within it. Such a tendency would push for a program aimed at the complete transformation of capitalist society, as well as insisting on the importance of direct action and democratic grass-roots organization.

THE DEMOCRATIC PARTY

Needless to say, it has proven to be extremely difficult to initiate a dynamic and viable new party in this country. As succeeding generations of revolutionary socialists have become discouraged by their lack of success, they have drifted toward reformism and realignment. Once having decided to accept the framework of the two-party system as given, these socialists have had to cope with the essential characteristics of Democratic party politics.

The Democratic party is primarily a coalition of competing interest groups held together by patronage, that is by the prospect of sharing in the spoils that go to the winning slate in each election. Questions related to substantive political issues are bound to be subordinated to questions of style in such a political party. Furthermore, key members of the corporate elite, and not the most liberal ones at that, play crucial and ultimately determining roles in the top councils of the party.

Recent events have further reinforced the links between the Democratic party and the capitalist class. As the Democrats have maintained their control of the House of Representatives and most state legislatures, substantial corporate contributions have been received by Democratic candidates. Capitalist politics is the politics of the practical, and, if the Democratic party continues to dominate key levels of government, then big business will orient toward it, despite the historic ties between business and the Republican party.

The Democratic party still encompasses within its ranks trade unions, black and Hispanic organizations, and mainstream feminist groups, as well as key corporate leaders. Because Democrats have provided the bulk of the votes required to pass progressive legislation, the organized working class has remained within the Democratic fold. Yet these limited legislative gains have primarily reflected the impact of mass movements and not the benevolence of liberal politicians.

Roosevelt and the New Deal responded to the tremendous upsurge of the unemployed councils, and then the CIO and the sit-down strikes. Only the militancy of the civil rights movement forced Kennedy and the courts finally to end legal segregation in the South. And, most recently, the Vietnam

War came to a close during Nixon's administration because of the massive wave of protests.

When working people are in motion, the power structure responds. Certainly the Democrats are more likely to seek to defuse the activist opposition through a policy that emphasizes limited concessions and cooptation, while the Republicans, or at least their rightwing, tend to press for coercion and repression. In spite of this difference in emphasis, the essential role of the Democratic party is to siphon off discontent during periods of unrest so as to leave the basic relationships of capitalist society intact and, indeed, to restrict the scope of any structural change, however reluctantly adopted.

Furthermore, once the activist base of a protest movement dwindles, Democratic politicians join with their Republican colleagues in dismantling the victories of the previous period. Under the impact of the protests of the 1960s and early 1970s, military spending was restrained and the provision of social services expanded. The recent push to an escalating arms budget began under Jimmy Carter, who also insisted on cutting back on social service programs. Reagan accelerated this reallocation of funds, but even then the House Democratic leadership, under Tip O'Neill, readily approved the thrust of Reagan's first budgets. Only as the 1984 elections approached did Congressional Democrats begin to denounce loudly Reagan's tilt toward the military and his tax breaks for the rich.

The essential nature of the Democratic party guarantees the failure of a realignment perspective. Realignment advocates soon discover the difficulties of transforming the Democratic party, but in the process they are themselves transformed. Since the New Deal, successive generations of socialists have dropped their commitment to independent political action and have wound up accepting the essence of the liberal outlook.

In a country such as the United States, with its weak tradition of socialist politics and the current isolation of the Left, the pressures to conform to the political mainstream are enormous. For many activists who have spent years and even sometimes decades in small ineffectual sects, the chance to influence decision makers has an overwhelming attraction.

Unfortunately, the price of conformity is high. In periods of mass activism, the movement presses against the limitations of the two-party consensus, and the progressive coalition comes under attack from the Left. For those who have become ensnared in liberal politics, a militant upsurge is perceived as a threat to the unity of progressive forces and to the Democratic party.

As a result, realignment advocates frequently devote their efforts during times of crisis to attacking the militancy of social movements. All too often, those who only a few years previously had been organizing from below for a more radical approach to politics become leading ideologues in the effort to convince the newly radicalized to stop participating in direct actions and instead to divert their energies to electing liberal Democrats. My study focuses on the distinct approaches succeeding generations of U.S. socialists have taken in relating to the two-party system. The chapters in Part 1 examine the socialist movement in its formative period, before World War I. During this period, independent working-class parties were being founded throughout Europe and, in this country, the Socialist party established itself as a serious alternative to the two mainstream parties. The following sections describe the experiences of two different groups of socialists who decided to enter the Democratic party, the Communist party in the 1930s, and the Shachtman tendency in the 1960s. In both cases, the decision to reject independent political action as a fundamental political principle quickly led to a cooptation of former revolutionary socialists into a reformist politics that basically accepted the liberal agenda for social change.

THE HISTORICAL PERSPECTIVE

Part 1 examines the positions taken within the early socialist movement on issues within the electoral arena. Marx and Engels frequently emphasized the need for working people to form their own independent party. As an exile in London, Engels enthusiastically endorsed the first independent electoral campaigns undertaken by British workers. In contrast, the Fabians, who were among the first socialists to develop a reformist perspective, argued that Britist leftists should remain within the Liberal party in order to capture it. The issue was resolved in 1900 when the Trades Union Congress joined with socialist organizations in launching the British Labour party.

At virtually the same time in the United States, socialist groups came together to form the Socialist party (SP). By 1912 the SP had 150,000 members and its presidential candidate, Eugene Debs, received nearly a million votes. Having succeeded in creating a mass base for radical politics, the SP sought to resist the intense pressures toward integration into the mainstream by sharply distancing itself from the two establishment parties.

The Communist party was started in 1921 from the fusion of two groups that had split from the SP. Communist policy remained firmly wedded to support for an independent mass electoral party until 1936, when the party opted to promote the Popular Front from within the Democratic party. Part 2 analyzes the ramifications of this decision, with special emphasis on the implications for Communist strategy in the newly formed United Automobile Workers. In order to protect the party's legitimacy within the New Deal coalition, party leaders found it necessary to curtail sharply the militant actions of its cadre on the shop-floor.

Part 3 traces the trajectory of an influential ideological tendency led by Max Shachtman, which had its origins in the Trotskyist movement. During the late 1930s, Trotsky argued that the formation of a mass-based labor party was an urgent necessity. Shachtman split with Trotsky in 1940 over the nature of Soviet society, but he remained a committed proponent of independent political action. By 1958, Shachtman and his sympathizers had become discouraged by their lack of success and joined the Socialist party. Once in the SP most of those in the Shachtman tendency quickly became fervent proponents of a realignment strategy. Indeed, several of the most well-known contemporary advocates of organizing within the Democratic party, including Michael Harrington and Irving Howe, are former members of Shachtman's organization, the Independent Socialist League.

NOTES

1. Walter Young, *The Anatomy of a Party* (Toronto: University of Toronto, 1969), p. 304; Gad Horowitz, *Canadian Labour in Politics* (Toronto: University of Toronto, 1968), pp. 257-58.

2. Horowitz, *Canadian Labour,* pp. 71-72; Gerald L. Caplan, *The Dilemma of Canadian Socialism* (Toronto: McClelland and Steward, 1973), p. 114. From 1933 to 1942 the only union to affiliate with the CCF was the Nova Scotia Mine Workers in 1938. This did little to help the party since both CCF and the Mine Workers had little strength in that province.

3. Caplan, *Dilemma,* p. 22.

4. Fritjof Capra and Charlene Spretnak, *Green Politics* (New York: EP Dutton, 1984), pp. 15-19.

5. Ibid, pp. 229-35.

PART I
THE MARXIST TRADITION

During the midnineteenth century, when Western and Central Europe began a period of rapid industrialization, those who worked in the factories and mines were disenfranchised from voting. As workers organized trade unions, they also called for universal suffrage. The existing political parties, with their close ties to the old feudal nobility or to the rising bourgeoisie, perceived these calls for working-class participation in governmental affairs as a direct threat to the established order.

For the industrial work force in these rigidly stratified societies, the demand for voting rights was frequently accompanied by widespread discussion of the need for an independent party. Only a distinct, working-class party could represent the interests of working people in the electoral arena, which was otherwise dominated by parties committed to defending the interests of different strata of the ruling class.

Karl Marx and Friedrich Engels formed their political perspective during this first stage of industrialization. They were also convinced of the urgent necessity of independent political action, but they extended the argument. A party based in the working class could aid the movement by projecting a coherent vision of a socialist alternative to the existing capitalist society.

Starting in the 1860s, independent parties, at least formally adhering to a socialist program, were established in most Western European countries. One exception was Britain, where most workers remained tied to the Liberal party. When this pattern began to crumble in the 1890s, Engels welcomed the first independent left-wing candidacies. At the same time, the Fabians, a group of reformist socialists, argued that socialists should concentrate their efforts on permeating the Liberal party with radical ideas. By 1900, the argument was resolved when trade unions joined with more radical socialists in founding the British Labour party.

In the United States, an independent electoral party was also late in developing. Although small socialist organizations contested elections in the period following the Civil War, it was only in 1901, with the formation of the Socialist party, that the Left became a significant electoral force. As the SP gained in strength, it protected itself from the pressures of cooptation by insisting on total independence from the Democratic and Republican parties.

2
MARX AND ENGELS ON INDEPENDENT POLITICAL ACTION

Questions of strategy related to electoral politics were crucially important to Marx and Engels. They believed that a significant socialist movement could only occur once the working class had definitively broken its ties with the capitalist political parties. In fact, by the time Engels died in 1895, mass-based social democratic parties were the general rule in most of Western and Central Europe. From the start, most socialists scathingly criticized progressive trade unionists who functioned within the more liberal bourgeois parties.

Marx and Engels consistently stressed the need for the working class to break totally with capitalist politics, and, indeed, their advocacy of an independent working-class party substantially contributed to an organizational split within the first international federation of working class and socialist groups, the First International.

GERMANY: THE FORMATIVE YEARS

Marx and Engels initially developed their political perspective in response to the German revolution. The 1848 revolution was a baptism of fire for both of the young revolutionaries, who were extremely disillusioned with its outcome. As the Prussian monarchy consolidated its authority throughout Germany, the middle-class liberals, organized into the Democratic party, became less militant in their opposition to the imperial regime.

When Marx arrived in London, he quickly intervened in an organization established to coordinate the activities of German exiles with those working class socialists who remained in Germany. This group, the Communist League, sought to use both legal and underground methods of resistance against the dictatorial regime of the Prussians.[1]

In 1850, Marx, acting for the central committee in London, issued an address to the League's members and supporters inside Germany. In this statement, he already emphasized the need for independent electoral activity. Further, Marx specifically rejected support of liberal capitalist parties on a "lesser evil" basis, that is, because of the immediate marginal benefits that might acrue to the working class as a result of the election of more liberal legislators.

> Even where there is no prospect whatsoever of them being elected, the workers must put up their own candidates in order to preserve their independence, to count their forces and to bring before the public their revolutionary attitude and party standpoint. In this connection, they must not allow themselves to be seduced by such arguments as, for example, that by so doing they are splitting the Democratic party and making it possible for the reactionaries to win. The ultimate intention of all such phrases is to dupe the proletariat. The advance which the proletarian party is bound to make by such independent action is infinitely more important than the disadvantages that might be incurred by the presence of a few reactionaries in the representative body.[2]

Soon after Marx wrote this address, the Communist League was effectively destroyed by widespread arrests, but the German working class continued to develop its own distinct forms of political expression. Although Marx and Engels initially posited the need for an independent working-class party on the basis of their experiences in the German revolution of 1848, their vision became a reality when Ferdinand Lassalle established the first working-class party in 1863.[3]

BRITAIN AND THE FIRST INTERNATIONAL

From 1850 onward, Marx and Engels found themselves in England, at a time when the British were the dominant world power. Skilled workers were forming unions and a strata of workers was able to gain higher wages. Marx and Engels lived through a period of relative economic prosperity in a country with a working class that did not appear to be receptive to socialist ideas. British trade union leaders were pragmatic business unionists with close ties to the Liberal party, the more reform oriented of the two capitalist parties. Socialists were few in number and isolated in influence until the great strikes of unskilled workers in 1889 and 1890.[4]

It was their work in the First International that led Marx and Engels to develop further their views on the need for a complete break with the bourgeois parties. At first the British unions worked harmoniously with the International with Marx as its leading member, but this loose working arrangement came to an end in 1870.

The intense faction fights that erupted then and that led to the destruction of the First International centered on the bitter disputes between the
anarchist and socialist tendencies, but a secondary split reflected the efforts
of the British trade union leaders to distance themselves from Marx and
thus to strengthen their ties with the Liberal party.[5]

Marx and Engels defended their perspectives from both of these points
of attack. In a resolution submitted to the First International and adopted
at its 1871 and 1872 congresses, Marx and Engels declared that "the working class cannot act as a class except by constituting itself into a political
party distinct from and opposed to all old parties formed by the propertied
classes."[6]

Until the 1870s, the issue was largely academic, but this was soon
changed as the British government was forced to widen the suffrage.
Leaders of the Liberal party quickly recognized the need to involve more
directly the trade union leadership in its activities. The key union in this
regard was that of the coal miners, at the time the most powerful union in
Britain. Coal mining was concentrated in a few areas of the country, and
the miners were therefore in an excellent position to influence the outcome
of elections in several parliamentary districts. In 1874, the first working-
class representatives were sent to Parliament, both of them national leaders
of the miners union. The two had run as nominees of the Liberal party, and
they continued to serve as loyal members of the Liberal caucus once
elected.[7]

Marx was indignant at this turn of events. In a letter to Wilhelm
Liebknicht in 1878, he wrote, "The English working class . . . had at last
got to the point where they were nothing more than the tail of the great
Liberal party, i.e. henchmen of the capitalists."[8]

Marx and Engels continually reiterated the strategic necessity for an independent working-class party, although the socialist movement hardly existed in England at the time and even though their persistence on this point
tended to isolate them from trade union activists and leaders.

These problems were particularly acute in London, where the Liberals
had especially close connections with local working-class leaders and where
virtually every worker eligible to vote did so for Liberal candidates. Engels
succeeded in gaining access to the newspaper of the London trade union
council, which was radical in politics (that is, it stood for social reform but
stuck within the confines of the Liberal party). The theme of Engels' articles
was the crucial importance of forming an independent working-class party
in Britain. "Everywhere the laborer struggles for political power, for direct
representation of his class in the Legislature—everywhere but Britain."
Engels soon decided to stop writing for this paper due to "the absolute lack
of effect produced by my articles."[9]

THE UNITED STATES

Marx and Engels viewed the United States and Britain as similar in that the historical development of both countries made it more difficult to form an independent working-class party than had been the case in the countries of Western and Central Europe. They were still certain that the working class would succeed in overcoming the barriers that existed in both countries to such a party.

In 1877, Marx responded with enthusiasm to a wave of railway strikes that spread throughout the United States. Although Marx thought the strikes would "be beaten down," he still hoped they "could serve as a point of departure for the organization of a serious labor party."[10]

After Marx's death, Engels continued to follow closely events in the United States. He recognized that "American conditions involve very great and peculiar difficulties for a steady development of a workers party." These difficulties included the ethnic diversity of the working class, the sustained prosperity then experienced by the United States, the lack of theoretical development within the working-class movement, and the plurality system of elections, which, as in England, "causes every vote for any candidate not put up by one of the two governing parties to appear to be lost, and the American, like the Englishman, wants to influence his state; he does not throw his vote away."[11]

Yet Engels considered all of these factors to be only temporary obstacles, which could and would be surmounted as objective conditions changed and as the working class developed a greater sense of itself as a distinct class. German Marxist émigrés could play a vital role in this process by aiding in the theoretical development of the working class, but only if they did not hold themselves aloof from the ongoing movement of the U.S. working class.

During the years from 1870 to 1890, the United States was characterized by a great deal of social and economic discontent, some of which spilled over into the electoral arena with the formation of local working-class parties. For a time during the 1880s, it seemed that the United States would actually precede Britain in breaking with the two-party system.[12]

Engels reacted with enthusiasm to these developments, and he urged socialists to become actively involved, although he was fearful that the small group of Marxists in the United States would isolate themselves by their insistence that any independent party adopt an explicitly socialist program from its formation. In a letter to Florence Kelley-Wischnewetzky, a U.S. sympathizer, Engels strongly urged socialists to support Henry George, then campaigning for mayor of New York City on a working class ticket. Although George was definitely not a socialist, his campaign was highly significant because "the first great step of importance for every country newly entering the movement is always the organization of the workers as an independent political party, no matter how, so long as it is a distinct workers party."[13]

Of course, socialists would continue to present their own perspective from within the Henry George campaign. They would "make it clear . . . that every movement which does not keep the destruction of the wage system in view the whole time as its final aim is bound to go astray and fail." This policy of critical support had proven to be an effective one, in that "all our practice has shown that it is possible to work along with the general movement of the working class at every one of its stages without giving up or hiding our own distinct position."[14]

Engels continued to urge the necessity of a complete break with the two-party system after the 1886 election. A year later he wrote in the U.S. preface to *The Condition of the Working Class in England*:

> In European countries it took the working class years and years before they fully realized that they formed a distinct, and, under the existing social conditions, a permanent class of modern society; and it took years again until this class consciousness led them to form themselves into a distinct political party, independent of, and opposed to, all the old political parties formed by various sections of the ruling classes.[15]

After the 1886 campaign, the local labor parties went into a rapid decline and the two major parties regained their dominant position. Engels believed that this development was a "temporary decline" in the movement toward independent political action. Writing in the last year of his life, he was still convinced of "the mass instinct that the workers must form a party of their own against the two official parties." The U.S. working class would overcome, in time, every obstacle to the formation of an independent party, even the sectarianism of the German Marxist émigrés, since "a country like America, *when* it is really ripe for a socialist workers party, cannot be hindered from having one by a couple of German socialist doctrinaires."[16]

Engels was too optimistic about the rapidity with which the U.S. working class would create and sustain a mass-based independent party. Nevertheless, Engels recognized that the development of such a party would be a lengthy process in the United States, as it would be in Britain. The crucial need was for the working class to begin to develop its own class policy, through the formation of an independent political party, and for Marxists to take part in every step of this ongoing process, although of course maintaining their own distinct perspective as revolutionary socialists.

CONCLUSIONS

To Marx and Engels, the formation of an independent party was a key step in the development of a class-conscious working class. Their views on this issue were consistent and unchanging. Marx and Engels sharply criticized those British trade union leaders who functioned within the Liberal party, that is, within the more progressive of the bourgeois parties. Their criticisms were voiced at a time when the socialist movement was an insignificant factor in British politics.

Marx and Engels believed independent political action was such a crucial component of a socialist strategy that socialists had to agitate consistently for it, even when this agitation isolated them from the most progressive elements of the working class. Yet Marx and Engels were also convinced that once the working class formed its own party, it was essential for Marxists to participate actively in it, whether or not it had adopted an explicitly socialist program. Of course, Marxists would consistently present a revolutionary socialist perspective from within the new party.

NOTES

1. Oscar J. Hammen, *The Red 48ers* (New York: Charles Scribners, 1969), pp. 159–68, 406–9.

2. Karl Marx, "Address of the Central Committee to the Communist League," in *On Revolution* ed. Saul Padover (McGraw-Hill, 1971), p. 117. The Democratic party represented the most radical wing of the petit-bourgeoisie. It was organized during the 1848 revolution, when it pushed for democratic government through universal suffrage. It was suppressed in the reactionary period after the failure of the revolution. Hammen, *The Red 48ers*, pp. 240–3.

3. Carl Schorske, *German Social Democracy, 1905–17* (New York: Russell and Russell, 1955), pp. 2–3.

4. Henry Pelling, *The Origins of the Labour Party, 1880–1900* (London: Macmillan, 1954), pp. 13–15.

5. Franz Mehring, *Karl Marx* (Ann Arbor: University of Michigan Press, 1962), pp. 458–62, 472–3.

6. Karl Marx, Frederick Engels, and V. Lenin, *On Anarchism and Anarcho-Syndicalism* (Moscow: Progress Publishers, 1972), p. 54.

7. Pelling, *Origins*, pp. 3–4.

8. Karl Marx and Frederick Engels, *Selected Correspondence, 1846–95* (New York: International Publishers, 1940), pp. 355–6.

9. Frederick Engels, *The British Labour Movement* (New York: International Publishers, 1940), p. 34; Marx and Engels, *Selected Correspondence*, p. 421.

10. Karl Marx, "From a Letter to Engels," in *On America and the Civil War* ed. Saul Padover (New York: McGraw-Hill, 1972), p. 42.

11. Karl Marx and Frederick Engels, *Letters to Americans* (New York: International Publishers, 1953), p. 258.

12. Yvonne Kapp, *Eleanor Marx* (London: Lawrence and Wishart, 1976), 2:193–95.

13. Marx and Engels, *Selected Correspondence*, p. 450.

14. Ibid, pp. 451, 455.
15. Frederick Engels, *The Condition of the Working Class in England* (Oxford: Basil Blackwell, 1958), p. 354.
16. Marx and Engels, *Letters to Americans*, pp. 269, 263, 258.

3
PERMEATION VERSUS INDEPENDENT POLITICAL ACTION

The formation of the British Labor party in 1900 marked a crucial turning point in socialist history. Britain had been seen as a bastion of the two-party system, and yet the Labour party soon became a major force in British politics. Often those who cite this critical breakthrough ignore the socialist forerunners of the new party. In particular, the Independent Labour party (ILP) first demonstrated the potential of working-class politics in Britain and then acted as a catalyst in the founding of the Labour party.

When the ILP was established in 1893, most trade union officials were solidly aligned with the Liberal party. The prospect of running independent candidates in opposition to the Liberals was a hotly disputed issue on the British Left. Key leaders of the Fabian Society were committed to functioning within the Liberal party. They hoped to permeate the Liberals in order to move that party toward a socialist perspective.

At the other pole were the many socialists who rejected the politics of permeation and who advocated an electoral policy independent of both establishment parties. Engels found himself in the midst of this debate, and he clearly opted for independent political action. Engels vigorously criticized the Fabians and staunchly upheld the path taken by the ILP.

The debate between these two positions is of more than historical interest, because the Fabian arguments for "permeation" so closely approximate the arguments of those contemporary socialists who aim at a "realignment" of the U.S. political context by working from within to transform the Democratic party.

Britain in the period from 1890 to 1905 was a testing ground for conflicting perspectives on electoral policy. When the British Labour party finally established itself as a viable mass party, it provided a clear proof that the working class can form its own class party, even in a country where the electoral system grossly discriminates against new third parties. In Britain, as in the United States, working people can break with "lesser evil" politics, but only as part of a process in which they develop an acute consciousness of themselves as a distinct social class with interests that can only be defended through their own independent party.

THE FABIANS AND THE 1892 ELECTION

Socialists became a significant force in Britain only after the massive strikes of 1889 and 1890, in which the London municipal gas workers and then the dock workers successfully organized and won recognition for their unions. This was the beginning of the "New Unionism" that aggressive, militant unions built along industrial rather than craft lines. In both strikes, key leaders were avowed socialists.

These victories gave a tremendous boost to working-class organization in Britain. This was particularly true in the north of England, where socialist groups grew rapidly in most of the major industrial cities. Initially, the British socialist movement was only marginally influenced by Marxist thought. Most socialist activists in the northern towns came out of the non-conformist sects, independent churches organized in opposition to the established Anglican church.[1]

As the socialist movement gained in strength, the idea of forming an independent working class party became more attractive. The 1892 elections to Parliament were the first in British history in which a significant number of working-class candidates ran outside of the two establishment parties.

These independent candidacies were sharply criticized by the Fabians. The Fabians were an organization of middle-class socialists, which had been founded in 1884. At first their politics were muddled, but a core group soon came to dominate, and they continued to guide Fabian policy for the next 25 years. The three key members of the Fabian nucleus were George Bernard Shaw, who later became a renowned playwright, and the Webbs, Sidney and Beatrice. The Fabians were explicitly hostile to Marxism, rejected out of hand the possibility of a revolutionary transformation of capitalist society, and emphasized the need for socialists to formulate specific measures of legislative reform. Fabian tracts on these reform measures were very influential on the British Left.[2]

Most Fabians lived in London, the area in which connections between the Liberal party and the working class were strongest. Throughout the east end of London there were radical workingmen's clubs, which advocated social reforms but remained strictly within the Liberal party. The Fabians were instrumental in promoting an ongoing alliance between these radical clubs and middle-class Liberal clubs, an alliance that successfully contested municipal elections. From the first London County Council elections in 1888, the Fabians acted as ideologues for this progressive grouping.

To the Fabian leadership, the London alliance of middle-class reformers and working-class activists was a model for the entire country. The Fabians sought to "permeate" the Liberal party, that is to organize a left caucus within it that could pressure the national leadership into accepting a program of social reform along the lines of the Fabian proposals.[3]

The Fabians were therefore exceedingly anxious to restrain working class socialists from breaking with the Liberal party. In the Fabians' 1892 election manifesto, Shaw succinctly defended the policy of permeation. He argued that the British electoral system, with single-ballot, plurality elections similar to those in the United States, acted to prevent the development of a new, third party.

The Fabians were concerned that a split in the "progressive" vote would ensure a victory to the Conservatives. Shaw held that "consequently if a third candidate comes forward . . . he is at once accused of a treacherous design to split the vote . . . and he is boycotted at the polls." Until the electoral system is changed so that it does not grossly discriminate against a new, third party, "the tyranny of our party system is complete."[4]

This clear statement of the supposed connection between the plurality method of voting and the two-party system preceded its official formulation as a sociological law by political scientists by decades.[5] Yet Shaw is not completely inflexible on this point. In certain districts, the working class was the dominant presence and thus could quickly replace the Liberal party as one of two major parties in the district. Shaw therefore did not exclude the possibility of working-class independent candidacies, but he argued there were "very few constituencies in which the Working Classes are politically organized enough" to sustain such a successful campaign.

For socialists in most of Britain, the electoral strategy should focus "on their chances of forcing the Liberal Associations to accept strong Radicals and Socialists as their party candidates." Of course, in most districts no such candidates would be running, and the choice would lie between a mainstream Liberal and a Conservative. The Fabian manifesto urged that "working men cannot be recommended to abstain from voting," but rather "it will be necessary in most cases to vote for the better of the two party candidates."[6]

According to Shaw and the Fabians, a voting system based on plurality elections forced those with a radical or socialist perspective to vote for the lesser of the two evils in all but a few districts.

ENGELS AND PERMEATION

While the Fabians chastised local labor parties for splitting the Liberal vote, Engels enthusiastically endorsed the break with bourgeois politics. In letters written to the German social democratic leadership soon after the 1892 elections, Engels noted that "the Liberals make concessions to the workers, either real or apparent," since "the Liberals know well that, if they wish to survive as a party, they must have the support of the workers." Nonetheless, "the true workers' candidates [are those] who act on their own account and who don't ask themselves whether they are running against Liberals or Tories." One independent candidate, Keir Hardie, was elected when the Liberal nominee in the district died during the election campaign. In Engels' view, "It is fabulous that . . . the workers' candidate, Keir Hardie, who took no money from the Liberals and who is not pledged to the Liberals, has turned a conservative majority of 300 in the last election into an anti-conservative majority of 1200."

In addition to Hardie, there were several other independent labor candidates, but Engels particularly noted that "in three localities where workers' candidates were soundly prepared, these candidates were defeated, but they have also caused the defeat of the Liberals."

By electing Hardie and by causing the downfall of three Liberal candidates, "the workers' party has given notice clearly and unmistakeably." The independent candidates of the working class "have given an advertisement of the future. This is hopefully the last election in which only the two official parties will be fighting it out. The next time the workers will come into consideration very differently."[7]

Engels was steadfast in his rejection of "lesser evil" politics. From his perspective, one of the highlights of the 1892 elections was the ability of independent labor candidates to demonstrate their power by providing the margin of victory for the Conservatives over the Liberals in three parliamentary districts. In doing this, the local parties had shown their commitment to independent political action and their ability to gain the support of working people. These achievements were of far greater significance than the marginal gains to be won through the election of Liberals to office.

Engels linked his praise of the independent candidacies of 1892 to a harsh critique of the Fabian policy of permeation. In a letter written to Karl Kautsky immediately after the 1892 election, Engels states,

> In our tactics one thing is thoroughly established for all modern countries and times: to bring the workers to the point of forming their own party, independent and opposed to all bourgeois parties. During the last election the English workers, for the first time . . . took a decided step in this direction; and this step has been surprisingly successful and has contributed more to the development of the minds of the workers than any other event of the last twenty years. And what did the Fabians do? . . . It preached and practiced: affiliation of the workers to the Liberals.[8]

Engels explicitly rejected the Fabian policy despite his awareness of the specific features of British elections and the possible barriers to independent political action that they might pose. An 1895 letter to Hermann Schluter specifically mentioned plurality elections and concluded that "everything is arranged for only two parties." Nevertheless, these obstacles could be overcome, since "once the workers know what they want, the state, the land, industry and everything else will be theirs."[9]

THE INDEPENDENT LABOUR PARTY

Keir Hardie's victorious campaign for a seat in Parliament gave a tremendous boost to the movement for an independent working-class party. In January 1893, local labor parties throughout the north of England came together to form a new party, the Independent Labour Party (ILP).

The Fabians sent George Bernard Shaw as their delegate to the convention. In a letter written on the eve of the convention, Shaw confided that "my present intention is to go uncompromisingly for permeation, . . . and for the bringing up of the country to the London mark."[10]

Once at the convention, Shaw continued to advocate the Fabian policy of working within the Liberal party. He vigorously opposed a motion that would have prohibited members of the Liberal or Conservative parties from becoming joint members of the ILP. Shaw told the ILP delegates that he was on the executive committee of one of the local Liberal clubs in London and "he intended to stick to it," further declaring that "there was a great deal of good to be done thereby." The motion was then amended to specify that only those who agreed with the platform could join the ILP, and the motion was then passed as amended.[11]

Engels greeted the formation of the ILP with considerable enthusiasm. He felt that "the formation of a third party was quite a good thing." Engels also continued to attack the Fabians for their unwillingness to break with the Liberals. Their policy of permeation consists of "not putting up Socialist candidates against the Liberals, but of fastening them on the Liberals. . . . That in the course of this process they either are lied to and deceived themselves or else belie Socialism, they do not of course realize."[12]

The ILP had a major impact on working-class politics outside the London area. With a membership of upwards of 5,000, most of them in the north of England, it was able to rally thousands of workers to the socialist cause. It also maintained close ties with leading figures in the "new unions," who zealously argued for independent political action within the Trades Union Congress.

Electorally, the ILP's record was more mixed. In its areas of greatest strength, in Yorkshire and Lancashire, hundreds of local officials were elected by the ILP. On the other hand, the ILP was unable to win a seat in Parliament. In the elections of 1895, the ILP ran 30 candidates in England and Scotland, none of whom, including Keir Hardie, were elected. Despite this, the party polled a substantial vote in the areas where it was strongest. Looking just at the 23 single-member districts the ILP contested, the new, independent party received 11.2 percent of the vote.[13]

Throughout this period, the ILP remained resolutely independent of the Liberal party. While the founding convention defeated a proposal to deny party endorsement to candidates of the two establishment parties, a general conference of the ILP instituted such a ban for the 1895 general elections. Furthermore, in October 1897, the ILP put forward its own candidate in a by-election in a miners' district, in direct opposition to a Liberal party candidate and to the leadership of the Miners Union, which was staunchly Liberal.[14]

Engels continued to support the Independent Labour party until his death, although he was disappointed at the slow growth of electoral support for the party. One of the last letters he wrote contains a doleful mention of Hardie's defeat in the 1895 election.[15]

The Fabians, on the other hand, remained very critical of the ILP. Beatrice Webb viewed the ILP as a "wrecking party" whose campaigns caused the defeat of her Liberal allies. A Fabian tract of 1896, again written by Shaw, denounced the "frivolous candidatures" of those who ran as independents in the general elections of the previous year. Such candidacies "discredit the party in whose name they are candidates because any third candidate . . . may involve in his defeat the better of the two candidates competing with him."[16]

Fabian hostility toward independent electoral campaigns was maintained even after much of the labor leadership had broken with the Liberal party. Although the Fabians were formally affiliated with the Labour party from its start, the Webbs continued to direct their energies toward aiding an inept clique of Liberal politicians who were renowned for their support of imperialist policies. Sidney Webb only became active in the Labour party in 1916, well after it had emerged as a significant electoral force.[17]

THE FOUNDING OF THE LABOUR PARTY

Hardie's defeat in 1895 was a major blow to the standing of the ILP. Although the party continued to win local elections in the north of England, its image as a national party was significantly undercut. Nonetheless, the ILP was able to act as a catalyst in the formation of a mass-based independent party. Several factors made this possible a scant five years after the 1895 campaign.

Independent Labor party members were to play an increasingly important role in the Trades Union Congress (TUC). Many of the key figures in
the great wave of strikes in 1889 and 1890 were socialists. Thus the unions
that had been built out of this strike wave were often led by officials sympathetic to independent political action.

As they became more prominent in the TUC, these "new unionists"
found that even the more conservative officials were looking with greater
favor toward an independent electoral policy for labor. Britain was in the
midst of an economic downturn during the late 1890s, a downturn that had
its greatest impact in heavy industry. The threat of prolonged unemployment convinced many workers of the need for radical alternatives to the
capitalist system.

Even more ominous were efforts by large employers to reverse the
gains of 1889. In 1897, the Engineering Employers Federation locked out its
employees and defeated the Amalgamated Society of Engineers after a bitter six-month battle. At the same time, unions in the railway industry failed
in a concerted drive to gain recognition.

These defeats at the workplace were reinforced by the government's
repressive measures. The courts greatly restricted a union's right to picket
during a strike. Serious discussions were also held in high government
circles aimed at making trade unions liable for the actions of their members
who were on strike. As it happened, this attack was later launched by the
courts through the Taff Vale decision.[18]

Trade unionists were therefore becoming increasingly receptive to
socialist arguments calling for independent political action. Yet it was the
ILP that finally catalyzed the formation of a mass, working-class party.
Although the ILP had always hoped to gain the support of the official trade
union structure for its politics, the idea of a loose coalition of trade unions
and socialist organizations acting as an electoral vehicle did not become a
major focus of ILP activity until after Hardie's defeat in 1895.

From then on, Hardie vigorously advocated this proposal, both within
the ILP and the TUC. In 1898, the TUC Congress voted to urge its members
to support "the working-class Socialist parties," but nothing concrete
developed from this motion. Shortly afterward, the Scottish TUC resolved
to call a special conference "to decide upon united working class action at
the next General Election."

Finally, success came at the 1899 TUC Congress, with the passage by a
narrow vote of a motion urging "the cooperation of all the cooperative,
socialistic, trade union and other working organizations . . . in convening a
special congress . . . to devise ways and means for securing the return of an
increased number of labour members to the next Parliament."[19]

It was this special congress, held in early 1900, that marked the founding of the British Labour party. Initially named the Labour Representation

Representation Committee (LRC), it was a loose coalition of organizations that had come together to sponsor jointly a list of candidates to Parliament. In the elections of October 1900, its first campaign, the LRC elected two of its fifteen candidates, one of whom was Keir Hardie.

Soon after this election, the Taff Vale case was finally adjudicated. Unions were made liable for the economic losses caused by the concerted activities of their members, such as strike picket lines, leaving unions open to enormous damage claims in legal suits. Taff Vale spurred most of the unions that had initially held back into active support for the LRC. The labor contingent in Parliament numbered 29 after the 1906 election, and the organization then formally renamed itself the Labour party.[20]

The ILP was remarkably successful in promoting the formation of a mass labor party. Unfortunately, in its eagerness to win the assent of the official trade union structure, the ILP leadership undercut the potential of the Labour party.

Throughout its history, the ILP had consistently emphasized its vision of an alternative society. When Hardie decided to push for a broadly based labor party, a socialist program went by the boards. At the LRC's founding congress in 1900, the ILP voted against an explicitly socialist plank proposed by the Social Democratic Federation. Once set along the path of social reform, it proved very difficult to imbue the Labour party with even the minimal commitment to socialism that has been characteristic of Western European social democracy. Only in 1918 did the Labour party adopt a constitution, much of it written by Sidney Webb, which contained the famous Clause 4 calling for "common ownership of the means of production."[21]

Decisions concerning the LRC's structure turned out to be of even greater significance than the initial formulation of a program. At first, the organization was strictly a federation of groups, with no provision for individual membership. Votes at the annual conference were based on the membership of each affiliated organization, with provision for bloc voting. Within the TUC, each union could cast its entire vote as a single unit, and this procedure was carried over into the LRC, and then into the Labour Party. Bloc voting enabled the chief officer of a union, often elected for life, to single-handedly control hundreds of thousands of votes at a Labour party congress.[22]

The initial structure, with bloc voting, but modified to allow for individual membership, continues in force to this day. Because of this, the Labour party is one of the least democratic of the Western European social democratic parties. Bloc voting has enabled moderate union leaders to overwhelm the votes of more radical constituency activists. By conceptualizing a labor party as the direct extension of the official trade union structure, Hardie and the ILP leadership guaranteed the dominance of the most moderate elements in the coalition.

The ILP was insistent on only one point; the new party had to be independent of the two establishment parties. Independent Labor Party delegates to the founding congress in 1900 sought to persuade the new organization that LRC candidates must "have no connection with either Liberal or Tory parties." The founding congress ultimately decided "in favour of establishing a distinct Labour Group in Parliament, who should have their own Whips and agree upon their policy." In 1903, under further prodding from the ILP, the LRC conference strengthened the organization's independence by requiring its candidates to "strictly abstain from identifying themselves with or promoting the interests of any section of the Liberal or Conservative parties."[23]

Yet even on this vital issue, the LRC leadership wavered. Ramsey MacDonald, LRC secretary, negotiated a secret deal in 1903 with the Liberal party leadership, under which key constituencies were parcelled out to one or the other of the two parties. The deal held for the 1906 election and to a lesser extent for the 1910 elections, but it came unravelled during World War I when the Liberal party began to disintegrate.[24]

Many ILP members were harshly critical of their leaders for being so willing to sacrifice basic principles for quick success. Beginning in 1907, the rank and file tried to pressure Hardie and other ILP leaders to take a more aggressive stance toward the Liberal party. After several years of intense disputes, a significant segment of the ILP quit to join with those in the Social Democratic Federation to form a new organization, the British Socialist party.[25]

CONCLUSIONS

The Fabians were correct in foreseeing significant obstacles to the formation of an independent working-class party in Britain. Elections by plurality vote produced outcomes in which smaller parties were blocked from gaining legislative representation proportionate to their share of the vote. A new party also had to overcome the previous propensity of working people to vote for the lesser evil from among the candidates of the two major capitalist parties. In a country in which the two-party system was a long established practice, a viable third party marked a sharp break with the past and would therefore have to overcome the inertia of tradition.

Engels was aware of these obstacles, but he believed that the British working class could, and should, form an independent class party. His support for the ILP was later vindicated by its success in acting as a springboard for the creation of the British Labour party. The ILP demonstrated the potential strength of a working-class party in Britain, and it also provided the organizational base for the many trade union activists who pushed the union leadership to break with the Liberals and to initiate a labor party.

Yet the ILP leadership was too willing to compromise on fundamental questions in its eagerness to gain official union backing for the formation of a mass-based independent party. If Keir Hardie and the ILP had been more patient, it is highly likely that such a party could have been launched on the basis of a socialist program, and without bloc voting, within a few years of the actual founding of the Labour party. Nevertheless, with all of its drawbacks, the emergence of the Labour party represented a major breakthrough for the British working class and a signal victory for the socialist movement.

NOTES

1. Henry Pelling, *The Origins of the Labour Party, 1880-1900* (Oxford: Clarendon Press, 1965), pp. 83-98, 125-36.

2. Norman and Jeanne Mackenzie, *The First Fabians* (London: Weidenfeld and Nicolson, 1977), pp. 109-12.

3. Phillip P. Poirier, *The Advent of the British Labour Party* (New York: Columbia University Press, 1958), pp. 30-33.

4. *Election Manifesto of 1892* (London: Fabian Society, 1892), p. 5. No author is ascribed to the manifesto, but the secretary of the Fabians later attributed it to Shaw. Edward R. Pease, *The History of the Fabian Society* (London: A. C. Fifield, 1916), p. 112.

5. The most influential formulation of this supposed law is Maurice Duverger, *Political Parties*, 2nd ed., (London: Methuen, 1959), p. 217.

6. *Election Manifesto of 1892*, pp. 6, 11.

7. Karl Marx and Frederick Engels, *Werke* (Berlin: Dietz Verlag, 1963), 38:384-93.

8. Karl Marx and Frederick Engels, *On Britain* (London: Lawrence and Wishart, 1954), p. 529.

9. Ibid, p. 538.

10. Poirier, *Advent*, p. 36.

11. Independent Labour Party, *Report of the First General Conference* (Glasgow: 1893), p. 13.

12. Marx and Engels, *On Britain*, p. 532.

13. Poirier, *Advent*, pp. 70-71; Joseph Whitaker, *Whitaker's Almanac* (London: 1896), pp. 135-44.

14. Pelling, *Origins*, p. 197; Poirier, *Advent*, p. 66.

15. Marx and Engels, *Werke*, 39:500.

16. Poirier, *Advent*, p. 66; *Report on Fabian Policy* (London: Fabian Society, 1896), p. 4. As an organizational statement, the 1896 document bears the name of no author, but it is attributed to Shaw in Mackenzie, *The First Fabians*, p. 231.

17. Mackenzie, *The First Fabians*, pp. 284-89, 397-98.

18. Pelling, *Origins*, pp. 195-201.

19. Ibid, pp. 203-5.

20. Henry Pelling, *A Short History of the Labour Party* (London: Macmillan, 1961), pp. 10, 18.

21. Pelling, *Short History*, p. 44.

22. Poirier, *Advent*, p. 81.

23. Pelling, *Origins*, p. 207; Poirier, *Advent*, p. 84; Pelling, *Short History*, p. 12.

24. Poirier, *Advent*, pp. 186-90; Pelling, *Short History*, p. 13.

25. Pelling, *Short History*, pp. 24-25.

4
THE SOCIALIST PARTY

The Socialist party provides the only U.S. experience of a socialist organization with a mass electoral base and genuine roots in the working
class. From the turn of the century until the advent of World War II, the SP
grew rapidly in size and influence. Largely through its efforts and those of
the Industrial Workers of the World (IWW), socialist ideas became a
significant current in U.S. working class culture.

For the Socialist party, the question of its relationship with the
Democratic and Republican parties was one of direct and immediate importance. The first years of the twentieth century were marked by the rapid
growth of the progressives, a movement made up of middle-class reformers
who organized as a pressure group within the two established parties.
Leading progressives were fearful of the rising tide of labor militancy and of
the growing strength of the SP. The implementation of a wide range of
social reforms, they believed, would undercut mass support for those proposing radical alternatives to the established order.

As the progressives succeeded in having some of their planks incorporated
into the platforms of the two major parties, the Socialist party found it
necessary to clearly demarcate the lines between itself and the reform movements, or the momentum that had built the party would be diverted back into
the confines of the two-party system. This problem was made more acute by
the dominance of the Center–Right forces in the SP, which stressed immediate
demands rather than long-run plans for fundamental change.[1]

THE FORMATION OF THE SOCIALIST PARTY

The SP was created by the merger of two small socialist groups. One
group had previously split from the Socialist Labor party, when its members

rejected Daniel De Leon's dictatorial control of that organization, as well as his "dual union" approach to the trade unions. The other was an amalgam of the remnants of Eugene Debs' American Railway Union and the German social democratic organization in Milwaukee.

These two organizations began merger discussions in 1899 and had still not completed them by the time of the national elections the following year. The two groups decided to nominate Gene Debs as their presidential candidate, in order to reach greater unity through this joint activity. The two groups considered the campaign to be a signal success, as Debs gained more votes than any previous socialist candidate. Yet Debs won only 87,000 votes or .6 percent of the total. The next year the two groups came together to form the Socialist party, which claimed 6,000 members but probably had significantly fewer.[2]

The decision to run Debs as an independent candidate was made despite the existence of significant differences between the two major presidential candidates. William Jennings Bryan, the Democratic candidate, ran on a populist platform of breaking up the trusts, opposing the colonial acquisition of the Phillipines and Puerto Rico and ending high interest rates through the coinage of silver. Bryan ran with the support of the Populist party, while his Republican opponent, William McKinley, ran with the financial support of the corporate interests. Despite these distinct differences, socialists nonetheless united behind Debs and denounced both major candidates as defenders of the capitalist status quo. Indeed, the SP decried Bryan for reflecting "the middle-class exploiter, who is unwilling to leave to the bigger fellows the spoils."[3]

Those who came together to found the Socialist party were sure that the time had come to launch a new, independent party. The turn of the century was a period of considerable economic instability and political turmoil. Many working people were looking for a radical alternative to capitalist society, and they were open to a more fundamental challenge to the existing system than that provided by either the populists or the progressives.

The SP was founded in 1901 with a small but enthusiastic core of supporters. It was launched without the backing of the official trade union structure, and indeed it consistently encountered the enmity of Samuel Gompers and the AFL hierarchy. Nevertheless, although small, the SP was never a sect. Even at its formation, it had a solid base of support in a few localities, primarily New York and Milwaukee, and it also had ties to local unions in those areas.[4] The party also succeeded because it countenanced a wide diversity of views under the umbrella of democratic socialism.

THE RISE OF THE SP

From its formation in 1901, the SP enjoyed a sustained period of rapid growth up to the outbreak of World War I. By 1912, its apex, the party had come to represent a significant force on the U.S. political scene.

The Socialist party always saw itself as the party of the working class. Thus its efforts to gain the support of existing unions were viewed as critically important. In 1912, leading officials in the Machinists, Ladies Garment Workers, Brewery Workers, and the Western Federation of Miners were members of the SP. In addition, a large number of Socialists were active in the Carpenters, Typographers, and the United Mine Workers. The SP's influence was felt in the AFL as well. Over 100 of the delegates to the AFL convention were SP members. At that convention, Max Hayes, a Socialist and a printer, challenged Samuel Gompers for AFL president and received nearly 30 percent of the vote.[5]

At its peak, the SP also had considerable success in the electoral arena. In 1911, the party elected over 1,000 local officials, including 56 mayors, most of them in small towns. Milwaukee proved the exception to this rule when, in 1910, it elected a Socialist mayor. On the state level, SP members were elected to office in 12 state legislatures. Generally, only one or two Socialists were elected at one time to these legislatures, but the SP contingent in Wisconsin numbered 14 in 1911. The party even surmounted the barriers of the plurality election system at the federal level when Victor Berger was elected to Congress in 1910. Of course, the presidential campaigns of Gene Debs were the capstone of the SP's electoral efforts. Debs did extremely well as his vote rose from 402,000 in 1908 to over 900,000 in 1912, 6 percent of the total vote.[6]

Yet the SP was not only a successful electoral vehicle with a substantial trade union base. Millions of people read its publications. In 1913, the socialist press had a circulation of 2 million readers. There were 323 socialist newspapers, most of them subsidized by local sections. Of these, 5 were English speaking dailies and 8 were foreign language dailies. No socialist paper had a greater impact than the *Appeal to Reason*, published in Girard, Kansas. At its peak, it regularly sold 760,000 copies an issue.[7]

Tens of thousands of people joined the SP as the socialist message spread throughout the country. By 1904, there were 20,000 members, which meant the party had quadrupled in size over four years. By May 1912, the party's high point, membership had increased to 150,000, making the SP a truly mass party. The SP not only grew in numbers, but it became a genuine national party. From its initial centers of support in New York and Wisconsin, the party expanded into the Mid-west and the West. By 1912, there were more than 5,000 members in Pennsylvania, Ohio, and Oklahoma, and sizable concentrations in California and Washington, as well.[8]

The Socialist party was unable to sustain its dynamic growth once World War I began. The tremendous upsurge of jingoism engendered by the war undercut the party, as most of its members held fast to their antiwar beliefs despite the shrill clamor of the press and a deeply divided people. After 1917, when the United States officially entered the war, the SP was the target of a concerted effort to destroy it at every level of government. Particularly in rural areas and small towns, members were subject to vigilante attacks and were fired from their jobs. Reeling from the intense repression, the SP was split by the impact of the Bolshevik Revolution, as its leftwing opted to form the Communist party. By 1921, SP membership had fallen to 13,500, less than one-tenth of the peak figure in 1912.[9]

Yet the tremendous growth of the SP before World War I demonstrates that viable third parties can be started with only a small activist core and a significant base of support in a few communities. This is not to argue that the potential for forming a viable third party exists at any time, no matter how isolated the Left may be. Obviously many third-party efforts have failed. Nevertheless, given a core of support, a willingness to respect a wide divergence in views, and an objective situation engendering widespread discontent within the working class, a small, tentative venture can develop into a mass party.

FUSION OR INDEPENDENCE

Although the Socialist party encompassed a broad range of viewpoints, there was virtual unanimity that the party should avoid any entanglement with the two establishment parties. The left wing of the party was especially fearful that those in the right wing would join with progressives on a local level to run a common slate of candidates. Such a development seemed most possible in Wisconsin, where the Milwaukee SP, led by Victor Berger, was building a strong electoral presence on the basis of a reformist program for social change. At the same time, Bob LaFollette and an insurgent alliance of farmers and middle-class progressives had taken control of that state's Republican party. The politics of fusion thus had a very real appeal in Wisconsin, and it was the determination of the left wing to block any moves in this direction, which accounts for the frequency with which this issue was debated within the SP.

Party policy on this vital issue was unwavering and forcefully stated. Gene Debs, the party's five-time presidential candidate, repeatedly denounced the Republican and Democratic parties as "the political wings of the capitalist system and such differences as arise between them relate to spoils and not to principles." The working class needed to "unite their class in the trades union on the one hand and in the Socialist Party on the other hand; that industrially and politically they must act together as a class against the capitalist class." Working people must "sever all relations with the capitalist parties." Those who vote for Democrats or Republicans "are guility, consciously or unconsciously, of treason to their class. They are voting into power the enemies of labor and are morally responsible for the crimes thus perpetrated upon their fellow-workers."[10]

That these statements by Debs represented the official position of the Socialist party can be seen by following the development of its platform and constitution on this issue. Debs first ran for president in 1900, and the platform for this campaign declared that "the working class can not, however, act as a class except by constituting itself into a political party, distinct and opposed to all parties formed by the propertied class." This formulation is virtually identical with the First International resolutions as written by Marx and Engels.[11]

To implement this policy, the SP adopted constitutional provisions that ensured the complete independence of the party from the capitalist parties and that also made it harder for opportunistic politicians to use the SP for their own interests. The latter problem was specifically addressed in the 1904 constitution. To prevent politicians from switching their official party allegiance in order to win reelection more easily, the constitution held that "any person occupying a position, honorary or remunerative, by the gift of any other political party . . . shall not be eligible to membership in the Socialist Party."[12]

A provision added to the constitution in 1912 went even further. The amendment required that every person nominated or endorsed by the SP had to be a current member of the party and must have been so for at least two years previous to the endorsement. Thus any current office holder who had been elected as a Democrat or Republican would have had to quit the office and then wait two years before becoming eligible for nomination to any office by the SP.[13]

An even more pressing concern was the threat of "fusion." SP locals were often urged to "fuse" for the duration of a specific election, that is to run a common slate of candidates with the more liberal of the two capitalist parties in their locality. With this in mind, the SP in 1904 insisted that

> no state or local organization shall under any circumstances fuse, combine or compromise with any political party or organization, or refrain from making nominations in order to favor the candidate of such other organization, nor shall any candidate of the Socialist Party accept any nomination or endorsement from any other party or political organization.

This statement of complete independence from the capitalist parties was accepted by virtually everyone in the SP. When proposed at the 1904 convention, it had such overwhelming support that it was passed without debate.[14]

The adoption of this constitutional ban on local fusion led to one serious confrontation within the SP on its relations with the capitalist parties. In 1905, Victor Berger endorsed a progressive candidate for judge in an editorial in the Milwaukee party newspaper. The candidate was known to be a Republican party stalwart, but the election itself was nonpartisan. It was therefore unclear whether Berger's move violated the party constitution, since he was not endorsing the candidate of another party.

In any case, Berger's endorsement became a focal point for debate when the left wing insisted that he be disciplined for violating the ban on fusion. Berger was suspended from membership on the national executive committee, and he was only reinstated when a slim majority of the party reversed this decision in a membership referendum. The Milwaukee local was eager to avoid further clashes on the fusion issue and did not endorse progressive Republicans after 1905, even in nonpartisan elections.[15]

The intense feelings generated by this controversy and the strong sentiment for disciplining Berger, even at the cost of a possible split in the party, are indicative of the determination of most members, especially those in the left wing, to preclude any overtures toward fusion with either of the capitalist parties. The issue became more critical in 1912, when both major parties introduced certain reform measures into their platform in order to woo away potential SP supporters. That year Teddy Roosevelt ran as the progressive candidate for president on an independent, reform ticket. Although the SP at this time was at the height of its success, its continuance as an independent working class party depended on its clearly enunciating its ideological and organizational independence from the capitalist parties.

The 1912 convention therefore went even further in guaranteeing the total independence of the party from the bourgeois parties. It extended the ban on support for candidates of the capitalist parties from the local and state levels to the individual member, and, in so doing, it also clearly included nonpartisan elections within the scope of this ban. For any member to vote for a candidate not nominated by the Socialist party or endorsed by the SP in the case of nonpartisan elections would constitute "party treason and result in expulsion from the party."[16] Obviously, this extreme version was unenforceable, but it does express the genuine concern of the SP to maintain itself as a distinct and independent party.

The necessity of complete independence was so widely accepted in the SP that it generated little debate during the prewar period of rapid growth. One minor exception took place in 1904 in the pages of the *International Socialist Review*, a theoretical journal allied with the SP. The journal was controlled by those in the center of the party who identified closely with Kautsky and the leaders of German social democracy.

In a 1904 article entitled "About Tactics," a Comrade Ignike posited a hypothetical case to highlight the "lesser of evils" argument. If in a

Southern manufacturing city one of the two candidates of the capitalist parties supported an end to child labor, while the other candidate opposed this and all other progressive legislation, then the Socialist section in this town should urge its members and supporters to vote for the more liberal candidate, since "socialists would not vote as socialists, but as fellow sufferers." To Ignike, the decision as to whether or not to support a candidate of one of the major parties was strictly tactical and could be justified whenever there were significant differences between these candidates and when the SP was not itself in a position to run a credible campaign.

In a brief note, A. M. Simons, as editor, stated his total opposition to this perspective.

> The maintenance of a class conscious political organization is the one hope of socialist success. To endanger that organization by temporary support of the candidates of a party, whose every principle is hostile to all that socialists want, would do the cause of socialism an injury infinitely greater than any possible, but very doubtful, good which any individual might be able to do for the workers.[17]

Simons' response represented the views of the great majority of the SP, and, because his views were so widely held, the issue could spark only a brief debate within the party.

CONCLUSIONS

The attitude of the Socialist party toward the two major capitalist parties continues to be of interest to socialists today because it provides us with the only case study in U.S. history of a socialist party with a mass electoral base. Starting at the turn of the century with a small core of support, the SP experienced a sustained period of rapid growth until the outbreak of World War I. This is not to imply that the overall policies of the SP during the prewar period can be taken as a model by contemporary socialists. On the contrary, the dominance of the center-right coalition led to the refusal of the party to confront the AFL leadership on the need to organize industrial unions in the new mass production industries, a refusal that significantly contributed to the relative weakness of the socialist movement and of the organized working class.

Yet even the dominant center-right coalition had to recognize the crucial importance to the Socialist party of maintaining its total independence from the two establishment parties. In a society in which class lines do not have the obvious and perceptible rigidity found in much of Europe, the tendency to fuse with liberal elements within the major parties could only be resisted through the continual reiteration of the need for a completely independent working-class party.

NOTES

1. Richard Hofstadter, *The Age of Reform* (New York: Alfred A. Knopf, 1956), p. 238; Ira Kipnis, *The American Socialist Movement, 1897–1912* (New York: Columbia University Press, 1952), p. 216.

2. Kipnis, *American Socialist Movement*, pp. 95–100; Congressional Quarterly, *Guide to U.S. Elections* (Washington, D.C.: 1975), p. 281.

3. Paolo Coletta, *William Jennings Bryan, Political Evangelist* (Lincoln: University of Nebraska Press, 1964), 1: 251-77; Socialist Party, *The Socialist Campaign Book of 1900* (Chicago: Charles Kerr, 1900), p. 137.

4. David A. Shannon, *The Socialist Party of America* (New York: Macmillan, 1955), pp. 6–24. At its formation, the SP also had sizable pockets of support in Chicago, where it never became a major electoral force, and Reading, Pennsylvania.

5. Kipnis, *American Socialist Movement*, pp. 339–44.

6. Ibid, pp. 345–46; Congressional Quarterly, *Guide to U.S. Elections*, pp. 282–84.

7. James Weinstein, *The Decline of Socialism in America, 1912–25* (New York: Monthly Review Press, 1967), p. 85; Kipnis, *American Socialist Movement*, pp. 247–48.

8. Kipnis, *American Socialist Movement*, p. 364.

9. Weinstein, *Decline*, pp. 140–45, 160–62; James R. Green, *Gross-Roots Socialism* (Baton Rouge: Louisiana State University Press, 1978), pp. 345–95; Kipnis, *American Socialist Movement*, p. 429.

10. Eugene Debs, *Writings and Speeches of Eugene V. Debs* (New York: Hermitage Press, 1948), pp. 127, 110, 129–30, 137.

11. Socialist Party, *Socialist Campaign Book*, p. 151; Karl Marx, Frederick Engels, and V. I. Lenin, *On Anarchism and Anarcho-Syndicalism* (Moscow: Progress Publishers, 1972), p. 54.

12. Socialist Party, *National Convention of the Socialist Party* (Chicago: 1904), p. 313.

13. Socialist Party, *National Convention of the Socialist Party* (Chicago: 1912), p. 156.

14. Socialist Party, *National Convention of the Socialist Party* (Chicago: 1904), pp. 153, 313.

15. Kipnis, *American Socialist Movement*, pp. 183–85.

16. Socialist Party, *National Convention of the Socialist Party* (Chicago: 1912), pp. 155, 202.

17. Ignike (pseud.), "On Tactics," *International Socialist Review* 5 (July 1904): 92–97. The comment of Simons is on p. 97.

PART II
THE COMMUNIST PARTY

The Bolshevik Revolution contributed to the disintegration of the Socialist party in the aftermath of World War I. For the first time, a group of revolutionary socialists held state power and in a country with enormous potential power. From the start, the Russian revolution had a decisive impact on existing radical movements. Lenin and the Bolsheviks sought to direct this enthusiastic support through the Communist International (Comintern). In the United States many of those in the SP's leftwing quit the party and formed several left-wing sects. In 1921 the Comintern brought these sects together into the Communist Party.

With the initial push to fusion, Lenin and the Comintern also instructed the fledgling party to propagandize for the formation of a labor party. Such a broad class formation would provide a conducive organizational framework within which the CP could act as a revolutionary pole. While the party's line continued to evolve over the following years, a consistent strand was total opposition to the two-party system.

In 1936, the CP broke with this tradition and decided to promote a Popular Front by joining the New Deal coalition within the Democratic party. The Communist party shifted from a focus on building a militant grassroots movement to consolidating its ties with progressive union leaders and liberal politicians. By 1936, the party had over 40,000 members and exerted considerable influence in important mass organizations, such as the newly formed CIO unions. The CP grew rapidly throughout the 1930s in membership and influence, despite its frequent shifts in political perspective. Because of this rapid growth, the CP's decision to abandon its commitment to independent political action had a major impact well beyond the confines of the Left.

No CIO union was more vital than the United Automobile Workers (UAW), which was organized from the grass-roots up. Within this highly politicized union the Communists constituted the largest grouping, but the party's supporters did not control the UAW apparatus. When the CP aligned itself with the New Deal, it lost its enthusiasm for militant strikes. Party cadre, who could have played a crucial role in leading continuing battles over corporate control of the workplace, were dissuaded from challenging the UAW's cautious leadership. In this way Popular Front politics facilitated the bureaucratization of the UAW in its first, formative years.

5
THE COMMUNIST PARTY AND ELECTORAL POLITICS

In 1936, the Communist Party decided to enter the Democratic party in order to promote a realignment of political forces within the two-party system. This decision represented a total break with its political past. From its formation soon after the Russian Revolution until mid-1936, the party had made several major shifts in its attitude toward electoral politics, and yet it had consistently urged the U.S. working class to break with the two-party system of capitalist parties. All this changed with the Popular Front.

The switch in electoral strategy was only one facet of an extensive revision in overall perspective. During the Popular Front period, the Communist party sought to legitimate itself within the New Deal progressive coalition. The CP downplayed militant politics and instead projected an image of mainstream respectability and patriotic fervor. These policies persisted from mid-1936 until the Stalin–Hitler pact of August 1939 and were even more in evidence during World War II. Thus when the Cold War polarized global relations at the end of the war, the CP found itself in a very difficult situation. After Earl Browder, who had led the party for 15 years, was purged from his post, the CP slowly moved away from its previous commitment to working within the Democratic party. This leftward shift led thousands to resign, thereby significantly contributing to setting the party on a downward spiral toward its present status as a sect.

EARLY YEARS

The Communist party was formed out of the left wing of the Socialist party, a left wing that was strongly influenced by syndicalist thought. Indeed, Big Bill Haywood of the IWW had been the Left's most important spokesperson until 1913 when he was forced out of the Socialist party.[1] The first leaders of the CP therefore became Communists believing that elections provided little more than a forum for revolutionary propaganda.

Charles Ruthenberg, the dominant figure in the early CP until his death in 1927, was a leader of the Ohio Socialist party before World War I. To Ruthenberg in 1912, the heyday of the SP, "The election of a mayor or any other party official is merely an incident in our work. It registers the increase in our strength, and that is about all."[2]

This attitude carried over into the newly formed Communist party, leading it to ignore largely electoral politics. A directive from the Third International prompted the party to drop this position and to enter the electoral arena. The Comintern's edict was consistent with Lenin's stance as he had consistently presented it. After the 1912 elections, in which the SP had scored significant gains, Lenin had been persuaded that these gains marked the "bankruptcy" of the two-party system in the United States, which "has been one of the most powerful methods of preventing the foundation of an independent labor, that is genuine socialist, party."[3] Lenin continued to hold these views after coming to power. He therefore twice urged delegations to Moscow to consider the building of a labor party as a strategic priority.[4]

In 1922, the Comintern intervened to end a bitter faction fight by deciding that the CP should emphasize its legal activity and stop romanticizing its role as an underground network. Furthermore, the Comintern required of the CP that "all energy must be directed toward building up a Labor party." This was a crucial task, since "if we succeed in building a large Labor party—at first with a moderate political program—it will be an event of historical importance."[5]

The 1922 Comintern statement established the framework for the CP's position on electoral strategy until 1928. Communist party activities in promoting a labor party were unsuccessful, with the highlight being a July 1923 conference for a farmer–labor party, which the CP first helped to organize and then took over and destroyed.[6] Nonetheless, the party continued to support the basic principle of creating a broad working class party, even after the 1923 debacle.

Ruthenberg, as the CP's general secretary from 1922 to 1927, repeatedly expressed his support for this strategy. In 1924, he declared that "the United Front has taken the form of a Farmer–Labor Party" in the United States. Yet the desire to cooperate with other working class tendencies in helping to form an independent party did not in any way imply that the CP would function within the two-party system. Ruthenberg held that "the capitalists foster the illusion that the Republican and Democratic parties, through which they maintain their class domination, represent the interests of the whole people. . . . The destruction of this illusion is part of our work. . . . From the foregoing it appears very clearly that under no circumstances can our Party support candidates on either of the old party tickets."[7]

Comintern strategy drastically changed at the Sixth World Congress in August 1928. By then, Stalin had solidified his control over the Russian Communist party (CPSU) and he had begun to implement his Third Period perspective on capitalist development. According to this theory, capitalism had recently passed through a period of relative stability and was entering a new period of economic crisis, in which the only alternatives were communism or fascism. The new line led to particularly vitriolic attacks on social democratic parties, which were denounced as "social fascists," that is supporters of fascism under the guise of their being proponents of social reform.[8]

In the United States, the CP denounced the New Deal as an essentially fascist program that could only gain working class support through the treacherous behavior of the trade union bureaucracy and the Socialist party. In April 1934, Earl Browder, party general secretary, argued that "Roosevelt, leading the present ruling class, stands for degradation, hunger, misery, oppression, fascism, war." He also insisted that fascism "must find indirect support. This it finds in the Socialist Party and the reformist trade union officialdom."[9]

The Third Period also led the CP to drop its efforts toward the formation of a labor party, and instead the party put itself forward as the only solution to the economic crisis. In an "Open Letter to Members" issued in 1933, the CP insisted that the creation of a farmer–labor party would only make the working class "an appendage to the petit-bourgeoisie." The only two choices confronting the United States were a reactionary trend to fascism or the "development of the Communist Party into a real revolutionary mass party."[10]

Communist ventures into ultra-leftist rhetoric ended in the latter part of 1934, when Stalin came to realize that Hitler represented a real menace to the Soviet Union. Comintern directives began to promote a working relationship with social democratic parties, a united front of the working class.[11] In the United States, the CP resumed its agitation for a mass-based farmer–labor party, which the Communists were eager to form with the aid of the Socialist party and other forces on the Left. During this period, even though the party emphasized the need to build a broad coalition of radicals and leftists, it remained hostile to Roosevelt and the New Deal.

Throughout 1935 and the first half of 1936, the Communist party vigorously argued for the formation of an independent party. Earl Browder called for "a decisive break with the two old parties." Furthermore, he added,

> to hasten the coming of Socialism in the U.S., it is necessary for the American working class to break with the old capitalist parties. To establish this political independence, the workers require a political party much broader in appeal and program than either the Communist or Socialist parties.[12]

The party had returned to a position similar to the one it had held from 1922 to 1928. The CP was clear that its policy during this period was inconsistent with any support for candidates running within the two capitalist parties. Accordingly, Clarence Hathaway, a leading communist functionary, chastised those comrades who "sincerely desiring to remain with the workers, decided there was only one thing to do: support the local Democratic candidates." But, he declared, "this is an example of right opportunism . . . which, instead of acting to break the working class away from the old capitalist parties, can only bind them more firmly to them."[13]

ENTERING THE DEMOCRATIC PARTY

As the 1936 election approached, the CP began to shift its position again. While the party still refused to support Roosevelt and instead nominated Browder as its presidential candidate, it centered all of its criticisms on the alleged evils of the Republican party. Communist election material emphasized and exaggerated the differences between Roosevelt and Landon, the Republican presidential candidate.

The CP election platform claimed that the presidential election posed the choice of "democracy or fascism, progress or reaction—this is the central issue of 1936." According to William Z. Foster, party chairman, the "1936 election constituted the sharpest class division in American history." Browder asserted "that the chief enemy of the peace, freedom and prosperity of the American people is the Republican Party." Indeed, "Landon's campaign, directed by Hearst from Rome and Berlin, raised every slogan of international fascism."[14]

The CP officially maintained its support for independent political action, but its agitational stance during the election campaign reduced this support to a perfunctory formality. The party made it very clear that it hoped for a Roosevelt election victory, and it defended its position by exaggerating the possiblity and dangers of a right-wing upsurge. Yet the Gallup Poll for June 1936, published at the same time as the CP's Ninth Congress, showed Roosevelt leading Landon by 53.2 to 42.2 percent. The final results were even more lopsided, 60.8 to 36.5 percent, one of the most sweeping victories in U.S. history.[15]

Within a month after the election, the Communist party formally entered the Democratic party. Browder told a party plenum that the Popular Front "will have to, for a time at least, include in at least most places forces outside and inside of the two old parties." Furthermore, the CP was opposed to the immediate formation of a nation-wide farmer–labor party, which had been a priority of the party as recently as Spring 1936. "Now more than ever there is a fear of prematurely forming such a party and thereby narrowing it down, leaving behind and outside serious forces."[16]

Communists soon became loyal members of the New Deal coalition. Browder held that the previous demand for an independent party was "no longer valid" because "the Farmer-Labor Party is taking shape and growing within the womb of the disintegrating two old parties." The result, he argued, was a "complete reconstruction" of U.S. politics in which the Democratic party was in the process of being transformed. Browder concluded that the CP should encourage unions and other mass organizations in which it was influential to engage in "systematic and organized activity within the Democratic Party (in some places, the Republican Party)."[17]

Eugene Dennis, a leading party official and a Browder protégé, found that there had been "a sweeping realignment in the two old parties," which could well allow the Popular Front to "take the form of a political federation, operating insofar as electoral activity is concerned, chiefly through the Democratic Party."[18]

The policy of the Popular Front, as it evolved from 1936 to 1939, did not just reverse the party's support for independent political action. The CP expanded its vision of those within the Popular Front to include Roosevelt and the New Deal. According to the *Daily Worker*, "the majority forces of New Deal democracy, labor and progressives, stand face to face with the forces of Big Capital." Browder also praised the New Deal because it "furnishes today the broadest framework, albeit a precarious and incomplete one, for the gathering of the full forces of the democratic front."[19]

These major shifts in the party position on electoral activity and the policies of the New Deal were embedded in an overall strategy designed to transform the CP into an accepted part of the U.S. political mainstream. Patriotic appeals became a mainstay of communist rhetoric. The party insisted that it was "carrying on the work of Jefferson, Paine, Jackson and Lincoln." During the 1938 election, the Communist party's chief slogan was "Communism is Twentieth Century Americanism." Browder even upheld the CP as "the most consistent fighter . . . for the defense of our flag and [the] revival of its glorious revolutionary tradition."[20]

A crucial aspect in the drive to gain respectability was an effort to defuse the hostility of the Catholic church toward communism. After the May 1938 convention, "a central point" in the party program became "our approach to the Catholics." The U.S. Catholic hierarchy had begun to move toward open criticism of the fascist states, so the CP concluded that "the Catholic Church itself is undergoing the most profound heart-searching and reorientation." Browder stressed that Communists "must get close to the Catholics, sympathetically closer to them, and assist them in their reorientation." Cooperative efforts by the party would "help to influence the integration of the Catholic community into the democratic front."[21]

A key element in the approach to the Catholic church was the in-
sistance by Browder and the CP that "questions of family and social
morality furnish no practical division between Catholics and Communists."
This fortunate coincidence in views arose because "Communists are
staunch upholders of the family. We consider sexual immorality, looseness
and aberrations as the harmful product of bad social organization. . . . We
combat them as we combat all other harmful social manifestations." Here
the Communist party took on the role of defender of civic virtue and moral
decency.[22]

WORLD WAR II AND AFTER

The Communist party dropped its advocacy of the Popular Front for
the duration of the Stalin–Hitler pact from 1939 to 1941. During these two
years, the party fought to keep the United States from engaging in a war
with the fascist powers. The CP again supported the formation of a
farmer–labor party and held that "neither of the two major parties, nor
their candidates, are worthy of the slightest confidence." To Browder,
Roosevelt had "betrayed the peace and prosperity of the American
people."[23]

As soon as Hitler attacked the Soviet Union, the Popular Front was
reinstituted, only this time in an even more extreme version. Browder now
found that Roosevelt's policies, including his "firm and continuing
cooperation with the Soviet Union," were indicative of "the essence of his
wisdom and genius." It was crucial that "the working class and all
democratic and progressive forces keep themselves firmly united around the
program of President Roosevelt." When FDR died, Eugene Dennis wrote
that the United States "has suffered the incomparable loss of its greatest
statesman."[24]

In 1944, the Communist party dissolved itself, as a gesture of patriotic
national unity, and became the Communist Political Association (CPA).
Robert Minor, a vice-president of the CPA, foresaw the possibility of a
postwar era of "prolonged world peace and a post-war economy permitting
full production and employment with a rising standard of living and social
gains to be won in orderly democratic procedures."[25]

According to Browder, this idyllic vision of the postwar period
depended on the continuance in power of those who supported New Deal
policies, the further consolidation of cordial relations between the United
States and the Soviet Union, and "the coming together of the most sober
and responsible national leaders of both capital and the trade unions with a
common program." Browder believed such an accord was possible because
a sector of the bourgeoisie is "consciously taking the progressive path; and

therefore the problem is no longer how to combat the whole bourgeoisie, but how to strengthen the progressive against the reactionary sector."[26] Eugene Dennis was even more explicit in his analysis. Communist postwar policy aimed at "a collaboration of classes," which would be "an integral part of national unity dedicated to bringing about a durable peace and an expanding post-war economy."[27]

Thus by the end of World War II, the Communist party had not only accepted the existence of the capitalist system for the indefinite future, but it had also adopted a policy explicitly advocating the creation and maintenance of a liberal coalition that would include much of the capitalist class.

When the CP's vision of postwar harmony foundered on the Cold War, Stalin had Browder replaced as party leader as a symbol of the end of the Popular Front period. The new Foster–Dennis leadership sharply attacked the previous policy of realignment, while it proceeded cautiously toward a break with the two-party system. Dennis declared that "it is necessary from now on to create the basis for organizing a major third party nationally." At first the CP limited itself to agitational statements on the need for independent political action. Although the party began to break with Truman in 1945, it did not fully swing behind the independent presidential campaign of Henry Wallace until after the Soviet Union established the Cominform in October 1947.[28]

This switch in line met with considerable resistance from within the CP. For most of the previous decade, the party had diligently pursued the Popular Front policy. Its decision to split with the Democratic party brought it into sharp conflicts with those liberals whom it had so assiduously courted. There was also notable opposition to the new policy among communist-influenced trade union leaders. When the party informed its most trusted and important union leaders that the party was backing Wallace, several vehemently objected, and Mike Quill, the head of the Transport Workers Union, quit shortly thereafter. Other communist officials agreed to endorse Wallace formally but made no effort to persuade their unions to back the Wallace campaign. Disaffection was also acute among secondary union officials, and many left the party over this issue.[29]

Resistance to the new line was not restricted to communist trade unionists. The open break with Democratic party politics in 1948 created a significant demoralization throughout CP ranks. From the end of 1945 to December 1946, the CP gained 20,000 members, thereby counterbalancing the losses it had experienced in the aftermath of Browder's expulsion. From December 1946 to August 1948, just before the presidential elections, the party's membership dropped to about 60,000, a loss of over 12,000 members in a year and a half.[30]

The dismay felt by many CP members during the Wallace campaign is hardly surprising. A party that consistently recruited and educated its members on the basis of its being an integral part of the liberal coalition could not directly reverse this policy without its members feeling betrayed. As John Gates, long-time editor of the *Daily Worker*, wrote in 1958 shortly after leaving the party, the decision to support Wallace meant that the CP had broken "with a policy which had united us with some of the most influential forces in political life and cut ourselves off from the mainstream."[31]

Of course, the Communist party had made drastic and unpopular shifts in policy before, such as backing the Stalin–Hitler pact and the purging of Browder. Indeed, the constant changes in party policy undermined morale and contributed to the rapid turnover in membership, even during the CP's heyday from 1930 to 1946. And yet the party had had enough momentum to overcome this and all of the other drawbacks inherent in its slavish adherence to the latest twist in Comintern directives.

By 1948, however, the overall context had changed. The CP had flourished despite its failings because millions of people saw the Soviet Union as a bulwark of the global antifascist alliance and an island of economic stability in the midst of the Depression. With the end of World War II and the advent of the postwar boom in the United States, illusions about the Soviet Union began to crumble, especially after the permanent occupation of Eastern Europe. In this setting and with the rising wave of anticommunist hysteria, the party could not overcome the shocks generated by its rapid shifts in basic policy.

The decline in membership during the Wallace campaign was followed by a further steady decline from 1948 to 1956. Yet, despite the loss in morale and the paranoia fed by McCarthyism, the CP held on to its hard core. Even in 1956, the party still had 20,000 members. It was the Khrushchev revelations of Stalin's terror and the Hungarian revolution that finally led to the disintegration of the Communist party. From early 1956 to late 1957, the party lost 85 percent of its membership. With 3,000 paper members, the CP had become an insignificant force in U.S. politics.[32]

NOTES

1. Ira Kipnis, *The American Socialist Movement, 1897–1912* (New York: Columbia University Press, 1952), pp. 417–18.

2. Charles Ruthenberg, *Speeches and Writings* (New York: International, 1928), p.30.

3. V. Lenin, "The Presidential Elections in 1912," *Communist* 7 (February 1928): 67.

4. Theodore Draper, *The Roots of American Communism* (New York: Viking Press, 1957), p. 280. Lenin's advice went to Lewis Fraina in 1920 and to the U.S. delegation to the Third Comintern Congress in 1921.

5. U.S. Congress, Senate Committee on Foreign Relations, *Recognition of Russia* (Washington: GPO, 1924).

6. Theodore Draper, *American Communism and Soviet Russia* (New York: Viking, 1960), pp. 43–48.

7. Ruthenberg, *Speeches and Writings*, p. 79.

8. Franz Borkenau, *The Communist International* (London: Faber and Faber, 1938), pp. 336–41.

9. Earl Browder, *Communism in the United States* (New York: International Publishers, 1935), p. 28.

10. Communist Party, *An Open Letter to All Members of the Communist Party* (New York: Central Committee, 1933), pp. 9–10.

11. Borkenau, *Communist International*, pp. 386–400.

12. Earl Browder, *What Is Communism?* (New York: Workers Library, 1936), p. 85.

13. Clarence Hathaway, "Problems in our Farmer-Labor Party Activities," *Communist* 15 (May 1936): 429.

14. Browder, *What is Communism?* p. 181; William Z. Foster, *The Crisis in the Socialist Party* (New York: Workers Library, 1936), p. 50; Earl Browder, *The People's Front* (New York: International Publishers, 1938), pp. 65, 102.

15. George Gallup, *The Gallup Polls, 1935-71* (New York: Random House, 1972), 1:25; Congressional Quarterly, *Guide to U.S. Elections* (Washington. D.C.: 1975), p. 290.

16. Earl Browder, "The Elections and the Popular Front." *Communist* 16 (January 1937): 25–26.

17. Browder, *People's Front*, pp. 161–63.

18. Eugene Dennis, "Some Questions Concerning the Democratic Front," *Communist* 17 (June 1938): 534, 536.

19. *Daily Worker*, November 4, 1938; Earl Browder, *The Democratic Front* (New York: Workers Library, 1938), p. 16.

20. Browder, *Democratic Front*, p. 93; Browder, *People's Front*, p. 105.

21. Earl Browder, "Mastery of Theory and Methods of Work," *Communist* 18 (January 1939): 18–19.

22. Browder, *Democratic Front*, p. 54.

23. Earl Browder, *Earl Browder Says* (New York: Workers Library), pp. 11. 14.

24. Earl Browder, *America's Decisive Battle* (New York: New Century Publishers, 1945), p. 19; Eugene Dennis, "Post-War Labor-Capital Cooperation," *Political Affairs* 24 (May, 1945): 422.

25. Robert Minor, *The Heritage of the Communist Political Association* (New York: Workers Library, 1944), pp. 47–48.

26. Browder, *America's Decisive Battle*, p. 20; Earl Browder, "The Study of Lenin's Teachings," *Political Affairs* 24 (January 1945): 4.

27. Dennis, "Post-War Labor-Capital Cooperation," p. 418.

28. Eugene Dennis, *America at the Crossroads* (New York: New Century Publishers, 1946), p. 32; Joseph R. Starobin, *American Communism in Crisis, 1943-57* (Cambridge, Massachusetts; Harvard University Press, 1972), pp. 159–73. The Communist International had been dissolved in May 1943 as a gesture by the Soviet Union to its Western allies. The Communist Information Bureau (Cominform) was established in October 1947, as the Cold War began to revive hostilities between the Soviet bloc countries and Western capitalism. Starobin, *American Communism*, pp. 54, 170.

29. Bert Cochran, *Labor and Communism* (Princeton, New Jersey: Princeton University Press, 1977), pp. 301–4.

30. Henry Winston, "Towards a Party of 100,000," *Political Affairs* 26 (January 1947): 67; Henry Winston, "For a Fighting Party Rooted Among the Industrial Workers," *Political Affairs* 27 (September 1948): 838.

31. John Gates, *Story of an American Communist* (New York: Thomas Nelson, 1958), p. 116.

32. David A. Shannon, *The Decline of American Communism* (New York: Harcourt Brace, 1959), p. 360.

6
THE COMMUNIST PARTY DURING
THE GREAT DEPRESSION

The success of the Communist party in the 1930s has often been presented as closely linked to the decision of the CP to enter the Democratic party and to support Roosevelt and the New Deal. As early as December 1937, Earl Browder, general secretary of the CP, argued that "the decay of the Socialist party in the past few years, and the rise of the Communist party furnish a neat test . . . of the relative validity of these two contrasting courses."[1]

Contemporary leftists who believe in working within the Democratic party continue to cite the CP of the 1930s as a model of success. Michael Harrington, for example, has contrasted the Popular Front of the CP with the critical stance taken by the Socialist party toward the New Deal, and he, too, concluded that the Communists' move into the Democratic party "allowed the American Communists to play a much more effective role in the U.S. than the Socialists."[2]

Immediate popular support has never been the primary criterion by which socialists have judged the validity of a fundamental shift in political perspective, but, in fact, these assertions can be challenged on their own terms at three distinct levels.

First, the CP dramatically shifted its political line several times during the 1930s. These shifts cannot be adequately understood as responses to either changes in the U.S. domestic political context or to changes in the attitudes of sympathetic forces within the progressive mass organizations. The CP was a loyal member of the Comintern, and, as such, its general political perspective was determined in relation to the perceived needs of the Soviet state.

Second, the evidence indicates that the success of the party, in terms of both the size of its membership and its influence, had little to do with its line at any given time. The CP gained in success because it was recognized as the U.S. representative of the Soviet government, and this attraction overrode in importance the specifics of the party position on domestic matters. Only with the Stalin–Hitler pact in August 1939 did a sharp shift in the line cause a significant setback to the fortunes of the party.

Finally, the SP did not experience a rapid disintegration of its organizational strength from 1935 to 1937 because of its continued criticism of the Roosevelt administration but because of a major split in the SP, a split that did not directly concern the attitude of the party toward the Democratic party or the New Deal.

THE PARTY LINE AND ITS SHIFTS

The argument that the Communist party gained considerable success during the 1930s because of its willingness to modify its programs and policies to fit the specific circumstances of U.S. political life implicitly takes for granted that the CP determined changes in its policies in accordance with the pressure of politics in the United States itself. Yet the most crucial and controversial issues confronting the party in the 1930s were its attitude toward electoral activity within the Democratic party and, closely related to this, its approach toward Roosevelt and the New Deal. When the record of the party and its shifts in line are examined, it becomes clear that it was not the domestic situation that determined CP policy but, on the contrary, the directives of the Comintern. Indeed, the specific timing of these shifts in line acted to undercut their impact as measures of political expediency.

THE CP AND ROOSEVELT

The decision of the Communist party to enter the Democratic party is often presented as imperative given the need to maintain links with the rank and file of the progressive organizations. Yet the real cutting edge was the attitude of the party toward Roosevelt and not toward the Democratic party.

In fact, the Democratic party was not particularly popular during the 1930s. Many Congressional Democrats consistently sought to block the administration's proposals for reforms, by allying with conservative Republicans. The widespread perception of the Democratic party as timid and unresponsive to the acute needs of working people allowed independent political parties to gain considerable success during the Great Depression. Both in Wisconsin and Minnesota, independent parties based on an alliance of farmers and workers won important state-wide electoral victories against the opposition of both major parties.[3]

Roosevelt was far more popular than the Democratic party itself. His image as a staunch fighter against the "economic royalists" enabled him consistently to run ahead of the Democratic ticket. In each presidential election from 1932 through 1940, FDR received considerably more votes and a higher proportion of the total vote than did the Democratic national slate for the House of Representatives.[4] (See Table 6.1) If there was a taboo topic, it was not the concept of an independent party of workers and farmers, which had considerable mass support, but rather the image of Roosevelt as the great liberal leader.

TABLE 6.1 Roosevelt Versus the Democratic Congressional Slate, 1932–40

	Roosevelt		Democratic Congressional Slate	
Year	Vote in Millions	Percentage Share of Vote	Percentage Share of Vote	Vote in Millions
1932	22.8	57.4	54.5	20.5
1936	27.7	60.8	55.8	23.9
1940	27.3	54.7	51.3	24.1

Source: U.S. Bureau of the Census, *Historical Statistics of the United States* (Washington, D.C.: GPO, 1975).

As it happens, the Communist party opposed Roosevelt in his first three presidential campaigns.[5] During the 1930s, the CP bitterly attacked FDR during both the 1932 election campaign and in the campaign leading to the election of 1940. Even in 1936, the party criticized Roosevelt and did not endorse him for reelection, although the party focused its attacks on the Republican presidential candidate, Alf Landon.

In 1932, William Z. Foster, CP chairperson, argued that, although Roosevelt had a veneer of liberalism,'' both he and Hoover "are representatives of the big capitalists of this country and both of them serve the capitalist class."[6]

Following the Stalin–Hitler pact of August 1939, Roosevelt was again condemned when he ran for a third term. Earl Browder, CP general secretary, insisted that "the surest way of wasting a progressive vote" was to vote for either Roosevelt or Wilkie, the Republican candidate. Indeed, Roosevelt, in repressing opposition to U.S. entry into the war, was setting up a "military dictatorship" and thus was introducing "all the trimmings of fascism."[7]

Obviously, during both these election campaigns, the CP sharply attacked a charismatic political figure. Despite this, the party grew rapidly during the time of Roosevelt's first campaign and victory. On the other hand, the CP was demoralized and lost members during the Stalin–Hitler period and the 1940 election. Since support for the pact represented a complete reversal of the previous effort to build an antifascist coalition, the surprise is not that a significant number of members quit but that most of the cadre remained loyal, if confused.

Only during the 1936 election did the CP soften its hostility toward Roosevelt. Yet even during this campaign, the party still did not endorse FDR and instead ran Browder as its own presidential candidate, this at a time when Roosevelt was at the height of his personal popularity.

Browder criticized the administration for "trying to pursue a middle course" and he held that Roosevelt's "course has been a series of retreats before the offensive of reaction."[8] But the party also strongly indicated its preference for Roosevelt throughout the 1936 campaign. It did this not by praising his administration but, instead, by its vitriolic condemnations of his Republican opponent, Alf Landon. Browder claimed that a Republican victory "would carry our country a long way down the road to fascism and war."[9]

The Communists' approach to the 1936 election completely reversed the verdict of public opinion. Roosevelt's landslide victory did not represent a vote against the reactionary views of his opponent, Landon, a colorless conservative, but rather reflected popular enthusiasm for FDR and the New Deal. Furthermore, despite the decision of the CP not to endorse Roosevelt in 1936, the party continued to grow in strength during this period.

Given that the party intended to enter the Democratic party, the most opportune time to have done so was before the 1936 campaign, not immediately afterward. Certainly Roosevelt's immense personal popularity at the time made it politically expedient for CP forces in trade unions and in other mass organizations to support FDR's reelection, if only critically. Yet only in December 1936 did the CP leadership openly announce its intention of working within the Democratic party. The timing of this decision was bound to minimize its impact as a measure of political expediency.

The specific timing of this switch in line is incomprehensible if we accept that the CP engaged in its Popular Front maneuvers primarily because of its desire to maintain its influence in progressive mass organizations. The mystery is quickly solved once we start with the proposition that every major change in its political perspective was undertaken by the CP in response to Stalin's perception of changes in the global situation, as relayed through the Comintern.

Browder has explained in his reminiscences that, while on a trip to Moscow, probably early in 1936, he and Foster were instructed to support Roosevelt. When Browder argued that Communist support could only hurt Roosevelt, Stalin agreed to allow the CP to decide its stance toward the 1936 election on its own, within the guidelines set by Moscow. The result was an election campaign in which the party focused its attacks almost exclusively on the Republicans and thus only indirectly indicated its support for Roosevelt.[10]

The position taken by the CP during the 1936 election is thus a key case in which party policy was not determined in response to the specific demands of the U.S. political scene but rather in response to the perceived needs of the Comintern and the Soviet state. Furthermore, in interpreting Soviet requirements, the CP adopted a position in the 1936 election that was bound to conflict sharply with its desire to avoid antagonizing non-CP progressives.

THE CP AND THE NEW DEAL

The attitude of the party toward endorsing the election of Roosevelt, as well as on the need for independent political action, can only be understood in the context of its views on the New Deal. Until June 1936, the CP had consistently condemned the Roosevelt administration. During the Third Period, Roosevelt's policies were declared to be "identical in their content with the measures of professed fascist governments." In Browder's view, "Roosevelt's program is the same as that of finance capital the world over. It is a program of hunger, fascization, and imperialist war."[11]

In the period from 1935 to mid-1936, the party developed a more sophisticated analysis of the New Deal as a shrewd attempt by Roosevelt, representing one wing of the capitalist class, to ward off demands for more fundamental reforms by agreeing to a much more limited set of reforms. Browder held that while "Roosevelt, of course, seeks to achieve fundamentally the same class objectives as his Right opponents," he is "basing himself upon different groups within the bourgeoisie." Roosevelt's aim was "to hold his mass base of farmers and workers," by offering "some tangible concessions to the well-to-do farmers and very niggardly concessions to the workers." A priority of the CP must, therefore, be "the problem of winning the masses away from Roosevelt."[12]

Only in June 1936, with the Ninth Party Congress, did this perspective change. The CP then came to argue that the New Deal was the program of liberal capitalism, and, as such, it was situated in the middle between the truly progressive forces and those of the reactionaries within the capitalist class.

The CP began to give critical support to Roosevelt and the New Deal, while continuing to argue for the necessity of an independently organized working class presence. To Browder, Roosevelt "hesitates and yields to pressure; he yields to pressure from the reactionaries, as well as labor." Thus while progressives, on balance, should support the New Deal, it was also essential for them to "create a strong political organization, an independent force, before they can force Roosevelt to stop surrendering their rights and liberties."[13]

The decision of the CP in December 1936 to enter the Democratic party did not lead it to modify its basic perspective toward the New Deal, but now the autonomous organizations of progressives would be organized as pressure groups within the Democratic party, instead of coming together within an independent farmer-labor party organized outside of the two-party system.

This overall policy of softened criticism of the administration, combined with clear indications of basic support, fit in nicely with Stalin's approach to Roosevelt in 1936 to 1937.[14] To Stalin, an alliance with the United States was of critical importance, but it was still unclear if Roosevelt was interested or whether the United States would continue its policy of hostility toward the Soviet Union.

All this changed after Roosevelt's "'quarantine,' the aggressor" states speech in October 1937. In this speech, FDR indicated that the United States viewed the fascist states as its primary enemy and that it would not remain neutral in a future war against Germany.[15]

From then on, the CP position became one of active support for the Roosevelt administration. The party began to talk of a new "Democratic Front," which would include the working class, the middle class, farmers, and the administration. As Browder wrote, "this New Deal wing under the Roosevelt leadership is an essential part of the developing democratic front against monopoly capital."[16]

Ironically, Communist acclaim for Roosevelt and the New Deal was at its height at a time when the administration was least willing to push forward with a program of social reform. From 1938 to the onset of World War II, the administration backed only one significant piece of progressive legislation, the minimum wage bill, and it was finally enacted in a highly attenuated form. This was a meager legislative record, given the continuing economic crisis, even when set against that of the first years of the New Deal.[17]

Furthermore, Roosevelt also reversed his minimal commitment to use the federal budget to counteract the Great Depression and to stimulate the economy. The administration sought to balance the 1938 fiscal year budget by sharply cutting social service expenditures, just as a further downturn in the private sector was dragging the economy toward a new slump. The result was a sharp drop in output and a further increase in the millions of people who were unemployed. The unemployment rate rose from an average annual rate in 1937 of 14.3 percent, the low point for the 1930s, to 19.0 percent in 1938.

Faced with another slide toward economic collapse, Roosevelt reversed his commitment to a balanced budget in April 1938, but only hesitantly and half-heartedly. Federal social service expenditures were restored for fiscal year 1938, but the harm to business confidence had already been done, and the unemployment rate averaged a high 17.2 percent throughout 1939. Only with World War II did the economy move out of the depression and into a period of full employment.[18]

Roosevelt's reversion to fiscal conservatism and his unwillingness to press for further measures of social reform led to a considerable decline in his personal popularity and that of the Democratic party as a whole. This drop in popularity can be seen in the results of the 1938 elections, when Democratic Congressional candidates received less than 50 percent of the total vote for the first time in a decade. As a result, the Democrats lost 75 seats in the House and 7 in the Senate.[19]

The Communist party was thus hardly bowing to public pressure when it enthusiastically urged a vote for every candidate who "wants to defend and extend the gains of the New Deal." According to the *Daily Worker*, just before the 1938 elections, "the people have no other choice except to inflict upon the Tory Republicans the resounding defeat our tradition of democracy and freedom require."[20]

The party sought to reverse the disillusionment of many progressives with the New Deal at a time when their confidence in Roosevelt had been eroded by his evident lack of concern for the interests of working people. The CP found itself in the anomalous position of extolling the Roosevelt administration after it had already lost its impetus toward reform and considerable popularity, as well, having previously attacked the administration when it had, in fact, undertaken certain limited measures of reform and when it was at the height of its popularity.

PARTY LINE AND PARTY SUCCESS

Until now, our analysis of the Communist party in the 1930s has concentrated on the contrasts between the evolution in the strategic line of the CP and the concurrent developments in the U.S. political situation. We now turn to an analysis of the impact these reversals in line had on the growth and momentum of the CP. There is no doubt that the CP gained in membership and in influence throughout the 1930s, but there is no convincing evidence that these gains depended on the specific stance taken by the party toward the New Deal or the Democratic party.

The CP's political perspective underwent several dramatic shifts during the 1930s, and only one of those involved support for Roosevelt and the New Deal. A closer look at this turbulent decade should enable us to test the extent to which the shifts in line affected the party's ability to expand its membership.

THE KEY SHIFTS IN LINE

Before this analysis can be undertaken, it is first necessary to fully delineate the major shifts in the position of the CP. During the decade 1930–39, the party went through three distinct phases in the development of its political perspective.[21] From 1930 through the last part of 1934, the CP was enmeshed in the Third Period, a time of shrill attacks on other socialists, as well as liberals, as "social fascists." The CP pursued a line of complete sectarianism, projecting itself as the "only solution" to the revolutionary crisis of capitalism.

Toward the end of 1934, this position began to be modified, and, during 1935 and the first half of 1936, the CP sought to work with the Socialist party in order to form a broadly based farmer–labor party as a radical alternative to Roosevelt and the New Deal.

The line changed again in June 1936 with the Ninth Party Congress. The CP greatly muted its criticisms of New Deal policies so as to avoid any conflict with the Roosevelt administration, although the party did not officially endorse participation within the Democratic party until December 1936. It is the three-year period from the Ninth Party Congress to the Stalin–Hitler pact that is so often presented as a model period that should be emulated by contemporary socialists.

COMMUNIST PARTY MEMBERSHIP

The most precisely quantifiable indicator of the success of the Communist party is the growth in its membership. The CP was remarkably forthright about its membership statistics from 1930 through 1936 and far less so afterward. We do have reasonable estimates up to December 1938, but for the following months up to August 1939, and the Stalin–Hitler pact, no exact information is available. Still from all indications party membership remained below the 100,000 mark over this period.[22]

TABLE 6.2   Communist Party Membership

	Year	Members
	1930	7,500
	1931	9,000
	1932	14,000
	1933	18,000
	1934	26,000
	1935	30,000
June	1936	41,000
September	1937	50,000
December	1938	82,000

Source: Note 22.

Table 6.2 demonstrates the rapid growth in membership achieved by the CP throughout the 1930s. This pattern was not significantly affected by the frequent and dramatic shifts in party policy.

TABLE 6.3 Growth in Communist Party Membership

Period	Annual Increase in Percent
1930–34	36.7
1934–36	24.1
1936-December 1938	33.2
1930–36	32.2
1930-December 1938	32.5

Source: Note 22.

The rate of membership growth observed in Tables 6.2 and 6.3 is quite consistent, and it strongly indicates that the ability of the CP to recruit new members and to grow in size had very little to do with the specific policies it pursued at a given time. Only CP support for the Stalin–Hitler pact and the abrupt reversal of its commitment to building an antifascist alliance brought a halt to the consistent growth in membership.

THE SOCIALIST PARTY IN THE 1930s

The success of the CP in its efforts to expand its membership is so often contrasted to that of the Socialists that a brief look at the record of the SP in this period is essential. Certainly the SP was more consistent in its basic political perspective. Throughout the 1930s, it called for the formation of an independent working-class party and criticized Roosevelt as a shrewd defender of the existing capitalist system. Despite its critical stance toward the New Deal, the SP did not blur the distinction between the corporate liberal policies of FDR and those implemented by the fascist states.

The most quantifiable indicator of the success of the SP during the 1930s is its ability to increase in size. Membership statistics from the SP can be readily compared to those from the CP. (See Table 6.4.)

The SP grew quite rapidly over the period 1930-34, more than doubling its membership. The party registered this success although it remained critical of Roosevelt, even during the first period after his election, when the new administration was most willing to undertake significant measures of reform.

Yet even during these four years, the growth of the SP did not match that of the CP.[23] Starting with a slightly smaller membership base in 1930,

TABLE 6.4   Socialist Party Membership

Year	Members
1930	9,736
1931	10,389
1932	16,863
1933	18,548
1934	20,951
1935	19,121
1936	11,922

Source: David A. Shannon, The Socialist Party of America (New York: Macmillan, 1955), p. 250.

the rapid growth in membership by the CP allowed it to surpass the SP by 1934. During the 1930s, those who became radicalized usually turned to the CP, not because of its specific policies — from 1930 to 1934, these could only be called sectarian and ultra-leftist — but because of the powerful image of the Soviet Union as the living model of a workers' state. The SP could just not compete with the romantic vision.

Beginning in 1934, the SP entered into a period of intense internal disputes, leading to a major split in 1936 and then a rapid decline in membership. Underlying this split was the antagonism of many of the new members, the "Militants," who were recently radicalized and considered themselves revolutionaries, to the "Old Guard," the previously dominant leaders who were reformists at heart but committed to independent political action. Already in 1935 the Socialist party was at a standstill, as the comrades "did little but fight one another."[24]

The Old Guard was particularly incensed by the statement of Principles passed at the May 1934 convention and then ratified by membership referendum. Although the statement reaffirmed that the "Socialist Party seeks to attain its objectives by peaceful and orderly means," it also proclaimed that should "the capitalist system collapse in general chaos and confusion . . . the Socialist Party, whether or not in such a case it is a majority, will not shrink from the responsibility of organizing and maintaining a government under the workers' rule."[25]

Left-wing Militants had been greatly affected by the February 1934 uprising of the Austrian working class. Here was a socialist movement that had finally shown the necessity of being ready to use force in order to defend basic working-class rights. Left-wing Socialists were convinced that a similar situation might well occur in the United States and that leftists had to prepare themselves for the coming conflict.

For those in the Old Guard, the Militants' position seemed to play into the hands of the Communist party. Although the old-timers rejected the revolutionary rhetoric of the young militants, they continued to hold on to their belief in the need to build an independent working-class party.[26]

This continuity in beliefs can be clearly seen in a letter from Algernon Lee to Karl Kautsky. Lee had been a leading figure in the SP during its prewar heyday, when he had been elected as a Socialist to the New York City Council. In a letter to Kautsky in 1935, Lee criticized the SP for having "within our ranks elements that waver between a shamefaced Bolshevism and the shallowest of bourgeois reformism." Yet Lee remained hopeful about the prospects for independent political action. "There will certainly be no real Labor party in 1936, but it is quite possible that such a party will be launched before the presidential elections of 1940."[27]

When the Old Guard finally quit the Socialist party in May 1936, the impact on the SP was quickly felt and devastating. From 19,000 members before the split, the SP rolls fell to 6,500 by February 1937.[28] Yet the SP was soon wracked by another split, which further decimated its ranks.

One of the controversial issues in the dispute with the Old Guard had been a proposal by the Militants to open up the SP to other revolutionary currents. A month after the final break with the Old Guard, the small band of U.S. Trotskyists entered the SP. This entry was one aspect of an international shift in line decreed by Trotsky, the "French turn."

The Trotskyists had only been allowed to join the Socialist party on the condition that they enter as individuals and that they cease to function as a disciplined tendency. Needless to say, the Trotskyists continued to operate as before, directing most of their efforts to denouncing Norman Thomas and the Militant majority. By August 1937, they were expelled for maintaining a disciplined faction, but by then they had succeeded in their goal. The Trotskyists took most of the SP youth with them, thereby giving the party another damaging blow to its morale.[29]

Certainly by 1937 the Communist party had become the dominant force on the Left. It could no longer be effectively challenged by the Socialist party, except in a few key unions such as the UAW. Still, the downfall of the Socialist party cannot be adequately explained by its critical stance toward Roosevelt and the New Deal. Rather, this downward spiral provides another instance of the tremendous demoralization caused by major organizational splits in which the bitterness engendered often leads to many of the participants becoming disillusioned with all political activity and organizations.

CONCLUSIONS

The decision of the Communist party to enter the Democratic party and to support the New Deal coalition reflected the imperatives of Soviet global policy and cannot be explained as one step in an evolutionary process by which the party successfully adapted its policies to the undoubted popularity of Roosevelt and the New Deal. The CP was a loyal member of the Comintern, and, as such, its basic policy perspectives were determined in Moscow, not in the United States.

Furthermore, the party's 1936 move into the New Deal coalition did not account for its rapid growth throughout the years of the Great Depression. Indeed, the CP's membership increased at a rate of more than 30 percent per year over the entire decade. This pattern of growth remained quite consistent despite the repeated shifts in party line.

The CP's success in recruiting new members stemmed from its close ties to the Soviet Union. While in the United States millions of working people were unemployed and destitute, the Soviet Union enjoyed full employment and economic growth. (Of course, millions of people in the Soviet Union were exiled to concentration camps, but that side of the Soviet paradise was generally kept hidden.) Also, after Hitler's rise to power in Germany, many U.S. citizens viewed the Soviet Union as a solid bulwark against fascism, while the Western powers temporized to avoid a confrontation.

The CP's record during the 1930s has often been compared to that of the Socialist party. In fact, the SP also grew rapidly until 1934, despite its sharply critical attitude toward the Democrats and the New Deal. Yet even during these years, the SP grew less rapidly than the CP. After 1934, the Socialist party dramatically declined in membership through a series of traumatic splits that were only marginally related to the question of whether or not to participate within the New Deal coalition.

Although the CP's decision to promote the Popular Front cannot account for its rapid growth during the Depression decade, it did have serious implications for its work in key arenas. In particular, working relations between the CP's cadre and other socialists, especially those in the SP, were acutely disrupted. This disruption was most damaging in the highly politicized CIO unions, such as the UAW. Communist policy during the Popular Front period has had one further important consequence. It has provided a historical model for socialists who have sought refuge in the liberal wing of the Democratic party.

NOTES

1. Earl Browder, *The People's Front* (New York: International Publishers, 1938), p. 14.
2. Michael Harrington, "The Socialist Party," in *History of U.S. Political Parties,* ed. Arthur M. Schlesinger, Jr. (New York: Chelsea Press, 1973), 3:2432.

For a similar view from someone who was in the CP and still identifies with its Popular Front policies, see Max Gordon, "The Communist Party and the New Left," *Socialist Revolution* 6 (January 1976): 11–47.

3. In Wisconsin, the Progressive party elected its candidate for governor in 1934 and 1936, and it also won elections to the Senate and the House of Representatives. The Progressives had their base in rural farm areas but also got significant support from the Milwaukee working class, which had a strong tradition of independent political action through its previous backing of the Socialist party. The Progressive party was not able to maintain itself as a significant electoral force through World War II. See Patrick J. Maney, *Young Bob LaFollette* (Columbia: University of Missouri Press, 1978).

In Minnesota the Farmer–Labor party was able to elect a governor from 1930 through 1936, and candidates on its ticket were also elected to the House and Senate. Congressional Quarterly, *Guide to U.S. Elections* (Washington, D.C.: 1975).

4. Roosevelt also ran ahead of the ticket in 1944. Furthermore, Democrats on the ticket consistently benefited from being able to run on FDR's coattails. The national Democratic slate of candidates to the House received an average of 53.0 percent of the vote over the four presidential election years of Roosevelt's victories. This compares to an average of 49.5 percent of the vote over the three non presidential year elections during Roosevelt's terms in office. U.S. Bureau of the Census, *Historical Statistics of the United States* (Washington: GPO, 1975), 2:1084.

5. Ironically, the only campaign in which the CP enthusiastically endorsed Roosevelt, the 1944 campaign during the war, was also his closest election victory. Roosevelt received only 53.4 percent of the vote, while the Democratic slate to the House garnered just 50.6 percent of the total vote. Congressional Quarterly, *Guide to U.S. Elections*, p. 292; *Historical Statistics*, 2:1084.

6. William Z. Foster, *The Words and Deeds of Franklin D. Roosevelt* (New York: Workers Library, 1932), p. 3.

7. Earl Browder, *The Most Peculiar Election* (New York: Workers Library, 1940), pp. 51–52.

8. Earl Browder, *The People's Front* (New York: International Publishers, 1938), p. 24.

9. Ibid, p. 24.

10. Earl Browder, "The American Communist Party in the Thirties," in *The Thirties As We Saw It*, ed. Rita James Simon (Urbana: University of Illinois Press, 1967), pp. 233–34.

11. Earl Browder, *What is the New Deal?* (New York: Workers Library, 1933), p. 17; Earl Browder, *Communism in the United States* (New York: International Publishers, 1935), p. 31.

12. Earl Browder, "United Front—The Key to Our New Tactical Orientation," *Communist* 14 (December 1935),: 1089–90.

13. Browder, *The People's Front*, pp. 78, 66.

14. By the time the Comintern introduced the slogan of the Popular Front in France in mid-1934, Stalin had been grudgingly convinced that Hitler was not likely to be quickly overthrown and that the formation of a left alliance within Europe was needed to block the spread of fascism. The U.S. extension of this proposed alliance with the social democratic parties of Europe was the overtures from the CP to the SP for joint work.

By early 1936, Stalin had come to see the necessity of a global alliance against the fascist states and thus the need for a rapprochement with the U.S. government. Franz Borkenau, *The Communist International* (London: Faber and Faber, 1938), pp. 380–98.

15. Franklin D. Roosevelt, "The Will for Peace," in *Nothing to Fear, Selected Addresses* ed. B.D. Zevin (Cambridge, Massachusetts: Houghton, Mifflin, 1946), pp. 110–115.

16. Earl Browder, *The Democratic Front* (New York: Workers Library, 1938), p. 16.

17. William Leuchtenburg, *Franklin D. Roosevelt, 1933–40* (New York: Harper and Row, 1963), pp. 261–63.

18. James McGregor Burns, *The Lion and the Fox* (New York: Harcourt Brace, 1956), pp. 313–28. Nonmilitary expenditures fell from $4.79 billion in fiscal year 1937 to $4.23 billion in fiscal year 1938 and then rose to $6.25 billion in fiscal year 1939. The source for this data, and that on unemployment rates in the text, is U.S. Bureau of the Census, *Historical Statistics* (Washington: GPO, 1975), 1:135; 2:1115.

19. U.S. Bureau of the Census, *Historical Statistics*, 2:1084.

20. *Daily Worker*, November 8, 1938.

21. This division into three distinct phases closely corresponds to the schema outlined by Browder in December 1937. Browder observed that CP policy toward the New Deal had gone through three periods nearly identical to those detailed below, except that Browder set the transition point between the second and third periods at the start of 1937, with the explicit decision to enter the Democratic Party, rather than in mid-1936, with the Ninth Party Congress. See Earl Browder, *The People's Front* (New York: International Publishers, 1938), p. 13.

22. For 1930 through 1935 the membership data are from William Z. Foster, *The Crisis in the Socialist Party* (New York: Workers Library, 1936), p. 39. His figures tally closely with other party sources and have the virture of internal consistency.

The June 1936 estimate comes from Browder's report to the Ninth Party Congress. Earl Browder, *The People's Front* (New York: International Publishers, 1938), p. 52. The figure for September 1937 is from Browder, *The People's Front*, p. 275. It agrees with the membership count for June 1937 given by Klehr using internal party documents. Harvey Klehr, *The Heyday of American Communism* (New York: Basic Books, 1984), p. 380.

For December 1938 the figure is from Earl Browder, *Social and National Security* (New York: Workers Library, 1938), p. 28. Browder reported to the May 1939 CP national committee meeting that the party was still short of its 100,000 member goal, and that he hoped that this benchmark could be surpassed by that September. The impact of the Stalin-Hitler pact in August 1939 led to a sharp drop in CP membership, so the goal was almost certainly not reached. Earl Browder, *The Meaning of the 1940 Election* (New York: Workers Library, 1939), p. 47. In a 1955 letter, Browder admitted to Theodore Draper that the party had never reached the 100,000 mark. Klehr, *Heyday of American Communism*, p. 367.

23. SP membership increased at an annual rate of 21.1 percent over the period of 1930–34, as compared to 36.7 percent per year for the CP over the same period.

24. David A. Shannon, *The Socialist Party of America* (New York: Macmillan, 1955), p. 242. The specific reference is to the New York States SP, but this contained nearly half of the total membership.

25. Murray B. Seidler, *Norman Thomas: The Respectable Rebel* (Syracuse, New York: Syracuse University Press, 1961), p. 130.

26. Seidler, *Norman Thomas*, pp. 125–65; Bernard K. Johnpoll, *Prophet's Progress* (Chicago: Quadrangle Books, 1970), pp. 135–77.

27. James C. Duram, "Algernon Lee's Correspondence with Karl Kautsky," *Labor History* 20 (Summer 1979): 432.

28. Shannon, *Socialist Party of America*, p. 249.

29. Constance Ashton Myers, *The Prophet's Army* (Westport, Connecticut: Greenwood Press, 1977), pp. 115–40. Myers estimates the Trotskyists entered the SP with 1,000 members and left with 2,000.

7

THE POPULAR FRONT AND THE UNITED AUTOMOBILE WORKERS

The Communist party reached the pinnacle of its influence during the 1930s, when for the first time in its history the CP became a significant factor in U.S. politics. In the estimation of the CP, trade unions were the key arena for Communist activity, especially the newly formed industrial unions of the CIO. Indeed, Communists were central to the CIO's tremendously successful organizing drives in the essential mass-production industries.

Yet, from mid-1936 to the Stalin–Hitler pact of August 1939, the CP held that the paramount need was to coalesce progressive forces into a Popular Front that could defeat the right-wing attacks on the accomplishments of the New Deal. After December 1936, the CP explicitly argued that the left should enter the Democratic party to strengthen the progressive elements within it.

The decision to orient toward the liberal wing of the Democratic party had a profound impact on the directives given by the party to its cadre in the CIO unions. For years, Communist policy had stressed the need to build a strong rank and file movement as the basis for militant unions. The CP had also sought to distance itself from the CIO bureaucracy, and its leaders had even been sharply critical of CIO president John L. Lewis. All this changed after 1936, with the CP's efforts to present itself as a "responsible" tendency within the progressive coalition.

Communist party policy within the CIO during the Popular Front period had three distinct but interrelated objectives. The party sought to enhance its influence and its membership within the new unions. With this as its base, the CP sought to strengthen its leverage within the CIO hierarchy and thereby to gain a more favorable hearing from Lewis and the other top CIO officials. Finally, the party prodded the CIO to use its clout within the Democratic party to push the administration toward a firm commitment to a global antifascist alliance with the Soviet Union.

Communist cadre on the shop-floor quickly felt the conflicting pressures inherent in Popular Front policy. The desire to gain credibility with the Roosevelt administration and to avoid the enmity of John L. Lewis inevitably led the party to oppose rank and file movements for more militant and democratic unions. This in turn tended to erode the authority of Communist cadre among the militant rank and file and eventually undermined the ability of the CP to withstand the attacks of other political forces within the CIO.

A complete analysis of Communist activity within the CIO would be an immense undertaking. Instead I have limited my analysis to one union, the United Automobile Workers, and I have primarily focused on one period, the year or so following the end of the Flint sit-down in February 1937. On December 30, 1936 hundreds of Flint's auto workers occupied a key GM plant which produced essential parts for the entire GM line of cars. The occupation lasted for several tense weeks, as the UAW brought GM to a standstill. Finally on February 11, 1937 GM finally agreed to negotiate with the union. The settlement provided that for the next 6 months General Motors would recognize the UAW as the sole bargaining agent for all workers in the 17 plants shut down by the strike.

With its victory at Flint, the UAW soon became the most dynamic and rapidly growing CIO union. It was also highly politicized as several socialist organizations gained adherents among the expanding number of UAW militants. Nevertheless, the Communist party quickly established itself as the most tightly organized and influential ideological grouping in the union.

Confronting the UAW were huge industrial corporations, the largest being General Motors. United Automobile Workers contracts with the Big Three, and especially with GM, were to become landmarks in the evolution of collective bargaining during the postwar period. Yet the pattern of labor-management relations was already being set at GM during the first formative period after Flint. Popular Front politics significantly limited the extent to which Communist cadre in the UAW could respond to GM's insistence on total authority over the pace of production.

Until the Flint agreement, the UAW was a small, ineffectual, and powerless force in the auto industry, but with recognition came legitimacy. General Motors made its continued recognition of the union contingent on the UAW's enforcement of the contract. Either the union leadership acted to police the contract against the rank and file, or direct warfare between union and corporation would be resumed. In the face of GM's ultimatum, the UAW leadership backed away from every confrontation.

Despite the timidity of the union's top leaders, rank and file discontent remained acute through the end of November 1937. Unfortunately, many of the shop-floor activists who could have provided leadership for a militant upsurge were Communist cadre, and, as such, they were trapped by the policies of the Popular Front. At critical moments, the Communist party decided to sacrifice the militant struggles of the auto workers in order to safeguard its legitimacy within the New Deal coalition. The party thereby facilitated the bureaucratization of the UAW, as it undercut the self-confidence and initiative of those on the shop floor.

INITIAL ORGANIZING

The 1929 crash found the Communist party at its most sectarian, in the midst of its Third Period phase. From 1928 until 1934, the CP denounced all other socialists and the entire trade union leadership as "social fascists" and entirely refused to work with them. Instead, the CP emphasized the formation of "Red trade unions," that is, unions outside of the AFL that were directly under CP control.[1]

In the auto industry, the Automobile Workers Union (AWU) was unable to gain a significant foothold in the plants, although the CP was instrumental in organizing large marches of unemployed workers in Detroit. While its direct successes were minimal, the AWU did provide the training ground for many of those who later became leading Communist cadre in the UAW.[2]

Soon after the Nazis consolidated power in Germany, the Comintern dropped its Third Period rhetoric and began to call for a coalition of forces on the Left. One consequence of this shift was the Comintern's decision to end Communist support for dual unions. As a result, the AWU was dissolved in December 1934 and Communist militants joined AFL locals.[3]

The AFL leadership had always ignored the auto industry as a place where industrial unionism across craft lines was inevitable. In response to the pleas of shop-floor activists, the AFL executive council reluctantly agreed to charter federal locals directly and placed one of their own organizers, Francis Dillon, in charge of them.[4]

Of course, the AFL still had no intention of putting substantial resources into organizing the unorganized, so the auto workers in the federal locals chafed under AFL rule. Rank and file activists prepared to take control of the union away from Dillon and to ally the UAW with the newly formed CIO. This was the situation in May 1936, when the UAW held its first convention as an independent union in South Bend, Indiana.

FROM SOUTH BEND TO FLINT

The delegates to the South Bend convention represented a union that was still a weak and disorganized force in the auto industry, one with a membership of less then 30,000. Nevertheless, the upsurge on the shop-floor was powerful enough to sustain a successful drive to democratize the union.

Communist party cadre were well placed to take a leadership role in the movement to establish membership control over the union's leadership. One of the key activists in this first insurgency was Wyndham Mortimer, a member of the CP, although he consistently denied it in public. A seasoned activist, Mortimer had begun organizing in the coal fields in the 1920s and had then come to Cleveland, where he worked in a plant producing trucks and joined the AWU. Mortimer was an extremely competent organizer, a skillful negotiator, and one of the most influential UAW leaders during its first years.[5]

Although Communists played a leading role at South Bend, they were not the only organized left-wing presence at the convention. Several key UAW leaders were former or current members of the Socialist party, and the SP maintained a caucus in the union.[6] Socialist party activists worked closely with Walter Reuther as he became an increasingly prominent figure. Reuther began his climb to power at South Bend by winning election to the union's executive board.[7]

In May 1936, Reuther had just returned from a two-year stay in the Soviet Union. Before his trip, Reuther had actively participated in the SP, but by 1936 he was only a nominal member. Nonetheless, Reuther's two brothers, Victor and Roy, continued to be active in the Socialist party after Walter had let his membership lapse.

A loose coalition of Communists and other left-wingers was in clear control of the South Bend convention. While leftists could strongly influence policy direction of the union, they were also well aware of the need to retain the support of the CIO and John L. Lewis. Thus, rather than elect Mortimer president of the union, as the Left could probably have done, the consensus candidate was Homer Martin.

Martin was a preacher who had worked for a short time in an auto factory in Kansas City. His rapid rise in the union stemmed from his skill as an orator. Unfortunately, Martin soon demonstrated his lack of strategic sense, his incompetence as an administrator, and his ineptitude as a negotiator.[8] He was a disastrous choice for president of the UAW, but he was not identified as a left-winger and he was highly acceptable to Lewis. The CP backed his election at South Bend, a decision they were soon to regret.

In early 1936, the Communist party was still committed to building an independent party of labor, although it had begun to hedge on this commitment. Communist and Socialist delegates joined in backing a resolution in support of independent political action. The South Bend convention overwhelmingly passed a statement pledging the UAW "to actively support and give assistance to the formation of a National Farmer Labor Party."[9]

Left-wing efforts around this issue did not stop there. When a delegate introduced a resolution placing the union "on record as endorsing Mr. Roosevelt for the next President," a spirited debate ensued. Opponents pointed out that such an endorsement would negate the call for a new, independent party. In a hotly contested vote, the resolution was defeated by a coalition in which Communists and Socialists were active.[10]

Needless to say, the CIO hierarchy was infuriated by the outcome of the vote. They were staunchly committed to backing Roosevelt's reelection, and they were adamant that the new, fledgling union not be allowed to undermine their electoral maneuvers.

Lewis's personal representative to the convention, Adolph Germer, privately told the UAW leaders that they had to reverse themselves and endorse Roosevelt or face the loss of CIO financial support for the drive to organize auto workers. Homer Martin then publicly declared that "I have just been speaking to Brother Germer" and that the defeat of the resolution would have to be rescinded "because of the effect it may have on the future of our Organization." The motion to support Roosevelt was then passed without further debate.[11]

The South Bend convention marked the high point of an effective coalition of left forces in the UAW working to promote radical politics within the union. This was soon to change as the CP engaged in a major shift in orientation and moved into the New Deal coalition. The Ninth Party Congress in June 1936 marked this historic switch, as the CP dropped its advocacy of independent political action and, instead, decided to build the Popular Front within the Democratic party.

With regard to the trade unions, the new line meant a determined effort to gain the goodwill of John L. Lewis and the CIO leadership. The party now sought to engage in "wholehearted collaboration" with CIO officials, and, Earl Browder, party general secretary, emphasized the CP's "great confidence in the strategical line of the CIO leadership and of John L. Lewis."[12]

The implications of Popular Front politics only became evident to the party cadre in the auto industry after the UAW signed the agreement of February 1937 ending the Flint sit-down. Until then the UAW had been a small, marginal union, without official recognition from any of the major auto corporations. With victory at Flint and recognition by GM, the UAW became an established union, with all of the problems inherent in that position.

Communist cadre had been instrumental in organizing the Flint sit-down. Mortimer had been initially sent to organize a base within Flint's GM plants, and he was soon replaced by Bob Travis, also a Communist and a protégé of Mortimer's. Travis relied on Communist activists in key plants as the core of the shop-floor organization needed to carry out a militant action. Although SP members such as Roy and Victor Reuther took leadership roles during the sit-down strike itself, Travis and other Communist cadre were of central importance.[13]

The victory at Flint greatly added to the standing of Communist activists among UAW militants. Party directives were therefore of considerable importance in the months following Flint, when the union's leadership was tested by the corporation and found wanting. Rank and file militants looked to the Communists for direction and, instead, found vacillation and timidity.

FIRST CLASHES

The first crisis was sparked by the strike against Chrysler in March 1937. Chrysler was less resistant to unionization than either GM or Ford, but it still refused to go beyond the GM pattern as set in the Flint agreement. The corporation would recognize the UAW as the collective bargaining agent for its own members, but it would not concede sole recognition to the union as the representative of all Chrysler workers.

Chrysler workers responded by occupying the plants and demanding exclusive recognition. After several days, the confrontation escalated when Michigan's Governor Frank Murphy, a liberal Democrat who had been elected with labor support, threatened to send in the militia to clear the plants. John L. Lewis then consented to an agreement with Chrysler based on the GM pattern.[14]

While the union claimed a great victory, Chrysler militants knew they had gained nothing by the strike. The agreement was unpopular with the rank and file, and it was only approved after Lewis made its acceptance a vote of confidence in his leadership. Many of the CP cadre in the auto industry were bitter about Lewis's role in negotiating the Chrysler settlement, and they loudly voiced their disagreement.

These criticisms of Lewis could not be countenanced by the CP. The Popular Front strategy placed tremendous importance on cooperation with the CIO leadership and on the presentation of the party as a responsible force for progressive politics. Browder strongly condemned the party's cadre in the auto industry, concluding that "some comrades were entirely wrong in thinking they saw intolerable compromises and wrong methods in the settlement of the Chrysler strike." It was "not our business to fall into any tendency of sniping" at the CIO hierarchy.[15]

Browder was also extremely clear about the control the CP would exercise over its members on this key issue. "We are a fully responsible Party and our sub-divisions and fractions do not independently take any actions which threaten to change our national relationship" with Lewis and the CIO officialdom.[16]

The Chrysler strike was the first instance of a recurring crisis. Auto workers were self-confident and militant after the victory at Flint, and they were more than ready to take on the auto corporations. On the other hand, Lewis and the UAW under Homer Martin were unwilling to confront the corporations beyond the extent needed to win corporate recognition of the union as a collective bargaining agent.

The focal point for this conflict within the union came to center on the tense relationship between the UAW and GM. The agreement ending the Flint sit-down had merely provided for bargaining between the two sides. This was followed by the first contract in March 1937, which established the guiding principles of the grievance structure, a key issue in future disputes.

In developing the union at the shop-floor level, UAW activists had sought to establish a shop steward system, in which each work group, roughly 15 to 100 people, chose a grievance representative who could settle disputes concerning the implementation of the contract.[17] If the union was to gain an effective voice in the determination of working conditions and production standards, a strong shop-steward system was an urgent necessity.

General Motors acted to undercut the workers' ability to police the contract by refusing to recognize stewards. Instead, it insisted on superimposing a new structure in which the number of recognized grievance officers was sharply reduced, and their authority was contractually defined and limited. A key provision of the March agreement established a system of committeemen to process shop-floor grievances. Each plant would have between five and nine committeemen, the specifics to be set at the plant level.[18]

The March agreement was negotiated by Wyndham Mortimer as UAW vice-president and chief bargainer. It was supported by the entire UAW leadership and by John L. Lewis, and then approved at a delegates conference of GM workers. The contract was a weak one, and its limitations reflected the reluctance of the UAW to challenge directly the control of the auto corporations over the production process.

Soon after it had been ratified, the March agreement had to be amended. The size of auto plants varied tremendously, so that the five to nine range for committeemen was soon found to be unworkable. One month later, Mortimer and Ed Hall, a UAW vice-president who was close to the CP, negotiated a new supplementary agreement. This April agreement was to be a matter of considerable dispute within the union. Unlike the March contract, it was implemented without ratification by the GM delegates conference and, indeed, on the sole authority of the negotiators, Mortimer and Hall, as well as Homer Martin as president.

Later, Mortimer was to defend the supplement as a clear improvement over the March package, which had gone to the GM delegates for approval. Certainly the number of committeemen was clarified by the supplement. It added one member to the grievance committee for every 400 workers over 3,600, in addition to the five to nine to which GM had already agreed.

While this removed the most objectionable feature of the initial contract, there was a substantial step backward as well. The April supplement specifically stated that shop stewards were not authorized to handle the grievances of other workers. Previously, in some GM plants where the union was highly organized, local management had implicitly recognized the steward system. The April supplement precluded this type of arrangement.[19]

The March and April settlements represented, in essence, defeats for the auto workers in their efforts to gain significantly greater control over their own working conditions. Committeemen who had to service 400 workers could not possibly remain in direct contact with all of their constituents. Unlike shop stewards, who were themselves members of the work department whose grievances they sought to uphold, committeemen would often have to act as another outsider adjudicating the disputes of those directly involved.

Of course, only an intense struggle could have compelled GM to recognize shop stewards. Whether the union could have triumphed in such a confrontation, given the balance of forces at the shop-floor, is difficult to determine in hindsight. In any case, it is clear that the UAW leadership, including those sympathetic to the CP, refused to organize a serious campaign to force GM to recognize the steward system.

Despite the hopes of Martin and Mortimer, the April supplement did not bring about a stable situation in the auto industry. General Motors acted to undercut the grievance system, even that based on the committeemen structure, by obstructing the quick settlement of disputes and by refusing to instruct its foremen to abide by the contract. The result was a massive backlog of grievances as the system came to a halt.

With working conditions deteriorating, the rank and file began to rebel. There was a widespread belief that the victory at Flint was being rendered meaningless by corporate obstruction. The UAW reserved the right to strike over contract violations concerning working conditions, should these violations not be satisfactorily resolved through recourse to the grievance procedure. Before such a strike would be sanctioned, the local membership had to approve the request for strike authorization by a two-thirds vote, and then the union's executive board had to approve the local's request.[20]

The union's strike authorization procedures were rendered meaningless by Homer Martin, who refused to approve local strikes over unsettled grievances. This left those in the plants with only one effective weapon: the wildcat strike. Workers were furious at GM, dismayed at the bureaucratic redtape of the official grievance procedure, and increasingly critical of Homer Martin's performance as UAW president.

The UAW of 1937 was not composed of apathetic or cynical members. Auto workers had seen that collective action could gain victories, and they responded to GM's maneuvers with wildcat after wildcat. Corporation officials claimed that there had been more than 200 quickie strikes in the four months following the March contract.[21]

General Motors responded to these strikes by threatening to refuse again to engage in collective bargaining with the UAW. In mid-June, GM president William Knudsen attacked the union for being unable to control its members. Wildcat strikes showed that the UAW was "not keeping the agreement," and, he claimed, this made the agreement a mere mockery.[22]

Martin and the executive board were nervous that GM would refuse to renegotiate the March agreement, so they were eager to placate the corporation. Thus the board replied to Knudsen's attack by condemning unauthorized strikes, and it warned its members that the "union will not support or tolerate" wildcats.[23]

The union's evident willingness to sanction corporation reprisals against those involved in unauthorized strikes put a damper on the first wave of shop-floor militancy. From late June to mid-November, GM was not hit by one wildcat.[24] Still the corporation insisted that the union bind itself in the contract to a tough policy on unauthorized actions.

On June 29, 1937, Knudsen wrote the UAW that GM would not reopen negotiations until the union stipulated that the corporation had unilateral authority to suspend any worker involved in an unauthorized strike. Martin quickly answered that "We are determined that unauthorized stoppages of work shall cease." Although he granted that the corporation should have the "right to fire as a point in attaining efficiency," Martin was not yet ready to concede to GM total control over discipline as a prerequisite to further negotiations.[25]

Unauthorized strikes were a focal point for debate within the UAW throughout the summer and fall of 1937. Given Communist influence in the union, effective resistance to Martin's policy of acquiescence to GM depended on the active support of the CP. Popular Front policies precluded this support.

As early as June 1936 and the initial shift toward the New Deal coalition, the CP made it clear that strengthening the Popular Front had a higher priority than support for the activities of a militant rank and file. Browder proclaimed that "the Communist Party is not stirring up strikes" and, indeed, that the "strike is a weapon of last resort, to which the workers turn only when the capitalists have blocked every other road of redress of their grievances."[26]

With this as its overall perspective, the party was bound to condemn wildcat strikes, and it did so, often and loudly. In the early summer of 1937, during the wave of wildcats in the auto industry the CP sharply disassociated itself from this expression of shop-floor militancy. The party official in charge of supervising the cadre in the auto industry, B. K. Gebert, wrote that "unauthorized actions must not be tolerated." Mortimer and Hall also publicly declared that "we wish to emphatically deny that we are in any way responsible, or in any way encouraged, unauthorized sit-downs."[27]

The CP was well aware that John L. Lewis condemned the wildcats and that he had urged the union to strictly adhere to the contract. The party had every intention of maintaining its good relations with the CIO hierarchy, and it required its cadre in the auto industry to pursue policies consistent with this goal.

The CP soon had to confront a more painful problem within the UAW. From the time of Martin's election as president in May 1936, key UAW leaders were convinced of his ineptitude and of the need to work around him. Martin responded by bringing into the union his own brain trust, recruited from the small sect of Lovestoneites.[28]

Jay Lovestone had been general secretary of the Communist party from 1925 to 1929, when he was expelled from the party as a right-wing deviationist during the CP's shift into its Third Period phase. Since then, the party had swung so far toward acceptance of the New Deal that Lovestone generally criticized Communist policy from the left during 1937 to 1938. Nonetheless, within the UAW the Lovestoneites were associated with the more conservative elements, and their actions as Martin's advisors were hostile to rank and file militancy.[29]

By early 1937, those close to the CP and to the SP were aware of the Lovestoneite capture of Homer Martin, and they were wary of the results. The first clash occurred in May when Martin exiled Mortimer to St. Louis, removed Roy Reuther as a Flint organizer, and took control of the union newspaper away from a CP sympathizer, appointing instead a member of Lovestone's group. Martin also began to red-bait his opponents, labeling all of them Communists, whether they were in fact sympathetic to the CP, or allied instead to the SP, or simply union militants without set ideological beliefs. Martin also organized his own caucus, the Progressives, with the clear intent of removing Mortimer from his position as vice-president at the upcoming UAW convention.[30]

For the Communist party, Martin's attacks were a disaster. The CP had no desire to engage in open conflict with Martin, who still had the support, if reluctant, of John L. Lewis and who also had considerable personal popularity among the ranks. On the other hand, the influence of the CP within the UAW would be destroyed if Martin and the Lovestoneites could successfully purge key members and sympathizers, such as Mortimer, from their positions of leadership.

The party resolved this dilemma by insisting on the need for an end to factionalism and for the retention of the entire existing leadership by the next convention. The CP avoided criticisms of Martin and instead focused its fire on the Lovestoneites as outside troublemakers.

In response to Martin's moves, CP and SP activists helped form the Unity caucus, which had as its program the end of factional disputes within the union. The Unity caucus proposed a slate of officers to the August 1937 convention that kept Martin as president and Mortimer and Hall as vice-president.[31]

The CP repeatedly insisted that it would gladly cooperate with Martin, but only if he would drop his efforts at a purge. Gebert, the party's key liaison with its auto cadre, wrote in the *Daily Worker* that "We Communists are for unity." He added that the program of the Progressive caucus was basically correct, and thus "on basic principles, there were no fundamental differences." The leadership of the Unity causus followed up this position by directly appealing to Martin for an end to this dispute, and, when this overture was rejected, they went directly to Lewis and the CIO with a proposal for a single, unified slate.[32]

MILWAUKEE AND AFTER

This is where matters stood at the time of the tumultuous Milwaukee convention of August 1937. The CP was convinced that it could only gain Lewis' aid in blocking Martin's drive to remove Mortimer from office if it demonstrated its "responsibility" at the convention. Local 155, which had a Communist leadership, presented a convention resolution that would not only have condemned wildcat strikes, but which would also have committed the union to disciplining those of its members who were involved in such strikes. In convention floor debate on a resolution reaffirming the requirement for executive board approval for local strikes, Mortimer strongly defended this procedure and declared that wildcats were "all wrong" and "absolutely out of order."[33]

Behind the scenes, Lewis personally intervened to prevail on Martin to accept a unified slate that retained Mortimer as a vice-president. Martin gained one victory when Richard Frankensteen was added to the list of vice-presidents. Frankensteen had helped to organize an independent union at Chrysler and had then led it into a merger with the UAW shortly after the South Bend convention. He was known as a nonideological pragmatist and as an enthusiastic supporter of the Roosevelt administration. He was to become one of the more moderate members of the UAW leadership in its early years. Shortly after the Milwaukee convention, Martin appointed Frankensteen to the newly created post of "special assistant to the president."[34]

While the Communist party continued to hold misgivings about Lovestoneite influence over Martin, it was also hopeful that CIO intervention

would provide stability within the union. Gebert was pleased that the
"outstanding builders and leaders of the union," such as Mortimer and
Reuther, had been reelected to the executive board. Furthermore, Martin
still had to be supported because he "condemns fascism and Nazism and
gives support to Loyalist Spain." The only fly in the ointment was the
"unhealthy and outside influence of Jay Lovestone."[35]

The truce in the factional dispute was to be a brief one. Within weeks
of the convention Martin resumed his attacks on the CP and sounded the
call for a throughgoing purge. It came quickly in late September 1937 when
Martin removed Bob Travis, a Mortimer protégé, from Flint and sent Victor Reuther into exile in Indiana. Martin then replaced an SP member as
educational director with one of his personal supporters.[36]

The CP was forced to respond or see its influence in the UAW be
destroyed. A *Daily Worker* editorial held that it was "unfortunate
that . . . moves have been made to 'purge' from leadership of the union
some of the outstanding organizers and builders of the union."[37]

Communist party leaders were convinced that Martin had reneged on a
deal and thus that he had to be persuaded of the need to cooperate with the
CP or face its active hostility. Yet the party still wished to avoid a head-on
battle with Martin. To meet these conflicting pressures, the CP adopted a
more critical stance toward Martin, although it continued to restrict its
criticisms within sharply defined limits. This ambivalent stance was
reflected in the attitude of the Communist party toward the crucial question
of UAW–GM relations, an issue that reached the crisis stage shortly after
the Milwaukee convention.

General Motors continued to demand, as a prerequisite to further
negotiations, a clear statement from the union granting the corporation
total authority to discipline those participating in unauthorized strikes. On
September 16, 1937, Martin conceded the point in a public letter to GM
president William Knudsen in which he stated "that the corporation will be
allowed to discharge, or otherwise discipline, union members known to be
or found guilty of instigating unauthorized strikes." In addition, Martin
promised that "the Union shall take effective disciplinary action" against
those involved in wildcats. The UAW leadership thereby threatened to expel
those militant workers who undertook direct action against GM for its continued violations of the existing contract.[38]

With a solid majority on the executive board, Martin's letter was passed
as the basis for negotiations to replace the March contract. Martin's letter
was tremendously unpopular on the shop-floor, particularly since it was
widely recognized that GM's drive to undermine the grievance procedure
had forced militants to call quickie strikes as the only effective means of
countering the corporation's effort to tighten its control over the pace of
production.

Communist response to Martin's September letter was very cautious. The *Daily Worker* remained silent until November 3, when Gebert wrote that "it is our opinion that the union paid too heavy a price when it agreed in September to accept provisions dictated by General Motors." The CP continued to insist on the need for shop-floor discipline, but it also called on the UAW to take a tougher stance in the GM negotiations.

By early November, Martin's team had negotiated a tentative agreement for a new contract with GM. In addition to a wage freeze and no improvements in the grievance procedure, it codified corporation control over disciplinary actions, as previously stipulated in Martin's letter.[39]

When word got out of the contract's provisions, opposition sentiment mushroomed. The forceful response to this proposed contract demonstrated the continued militancy of UAW members. It also marked the first significant break in the Unity Caucus.

During the first part of 1937, relations between CP and SP activists in the union had been relatively close. Although relations at the national level between the two organizations were, at best, cool, Communists worked smoothly with Socialist party members and sympathizers within the UAW. To the Communists, SP activists in the auto industry were "Socialists who were not infected with the poison of Trotskyism or influenced to any large extent by the sectarianism of the militant Socialists."[40]

For its part, the SP caucus in the auto industry was very skeptical of CP intentions, but it was also convinced of the need to maintain a tactical alliance with the CP in order to project a credible alternative to the weak and ineffective policies of Homer Martin. Nevertheless, Socialists were disenchanted with the Communist party's role in the UAW. According to the SP, Communist attacks on wildcats were "hardly distinguishable from Martin's."[41]

Walter Reuther played a key role in holding the Unity caucus together. Until the Milwaukee convention, Reuther was extremely close to the CP. The party's rejection of independent political action corresponded to Reuther's own pragmatic attitude toward Roosevelt and the New Deal. Furthermore, Reuther was well aware of the CP's considerable influence within the UAW and of the benefits to be gained from its support for his future campaigns for higher office.[42]

While his flirtations with the CP raised considerable suspicion within the SP auto caucus,[43] the SP continued to align itself with Reuther in the union's internal disputes. Thus Reuther was in a unique position to act as liaison between the CP and the SP during the first months of the battle against Martin and the Lovestoneites.

The tentative agreement of November 1937 led Reuther to end this role. He quickly joined the opposition to the proposed contact and assailed its inadequacies. The *West Side Conveyor*, the newspaper of Local 174,

Reuther's home local, attacked Martin's willingness to accede to GM's demand for total authority to discipline unauthorized strikers as a precondition to bargaining. The tentative agreement was also criticized for not including the shop steward system as an integral element of the grievance procedure.[44]

On November 13 and 14, 300 delegates from GM locals convened to discuss the proposed contract. As the delegates entered the meeting hall in Detroit, they were handed copies of the *Conveyor* denouncing the agreement.[45] During the first day of the conference, delegate after delegate attacked the provisions of the proposed contract and urged its rejection. Finally, Martin sought to regain control of the conference by announcing that he also opposed the tentative agreement and that the union's negotiating team would return to the bargaining table to gain a stronger contract.

Following a quick and unanimous vote to turn down the proposed contract, debate turned to the need for a new strategy to force GM off dead center. Communist cadre were cautious in their proposals for future actions. Bob Travis, unofficially representing the CP at the delegates conference, joined with other delegates in rejecting the tentative contract, but he limited his plan for the immediate future to a publicity campaign aimed at GM's contract violations, with the intention of gaining greater public support for further actions.

For the Reuthers, the delegates conference provided the ideal way for them to be seen as the leadership of the militant opposition. Roy Reuther insisted that "we have got to put that old militant front on this union." Walter then declared that "the important task that we face is to reestablish ourselves with General Motors on the same sort of relationship we had back during the strike period."

Walter Reuther then proposed that the union call short, authorized strikes at key plants. This would demonstrate to the corporation that the union had "disciplined power" and would force it to negotiate seriously. Needless to say, Martin quickly buried any plans for a militant campaign against GM.[46]

Fear of reprisals against unauthorized strikers had kept the lid on shop-floor discontent throughout the summer and into the fall of 1937. When the GM delegates rejected the tentative agreement, they lifted the lid. Rank and file activists were convinced that the union was once again committed to defending its members against corporate reprisals, rather than sanctioning them. The stage was set for another confrontation with General Motors, and it came at the Fisher Body Plant in Pontiac, Michigan.

THE PONTIAC WILDCAT

Pontiac Fisher Body was one of the most militant and well organized plants in the GM complex. Its normal workforce was 7,500, but 1,350 workers were laid off as of November 1937. In large part, these lay-offs stemmed from GM's decision to shift some of the work normally undertaken at Pontiac to another Fisher Body plant in Linden, New Jersey. The Linden facility was still unorganized by the union, and GM intended to keep it that way by refusing to allow Pontiac workers to follow the switch in work sites.[47]

The Pontiac local had objected to the lay-offs and had proposed a sharply reduced work week as an alternative. Local management refused to consider the union's plan or to negotiate otherwise on the lay-offs. Pontiac Fisher Body workers also believed that GM was speeding up the pace of production as it laid off workers. Grievances at the plant piled up, as the grievance procedure ground to a halt in the face of the corporation's hard line.[48]

The Pontiac plant was a tinderbox ready to explode. Yet as of early summer, the threat of being fired had acted as an effective deterrent to wildcat strikes. When the tentative contract came up for a vote at the GM delegates conference, the ranks realized that the time to strike back at GM had arrived.

Delegates from the Pontiac local actively participated in the drive to defeat the contract. One Pontiac delegate told the GM conference that "I believe real militancy on the part of this organization is the only thing which will bring them [GM] to terms."[49]

When word of the GM delegates' decision to reject the contract reached Pontiac, a suburb of Detroit, workers at the Fisher Body Plant reacted instantaneously. On Monday, November 15, at 8:45 P.M., the evening shift refused to work, and 2,500 workers occupied the plant in a sitdown. The strike was short, less than 12 hours, but at first it appeared to have been successful. Local management agreed to negotiate lay-off procedures with the union.[50]

The victory was short-lived. On Wednesday morning, November 17, GM dismissed four leading activists in the plant, including George Method, chairman of the Fisher Bargaining Committee and a Communist sympathizer. The four were accused of leading the wildcat, and the corporation insisted that Martin's September letter gave it the undisputed authority to discipline those who instigated unauthorized strikes. General Motors maintained this despite the defeat of the tentative agreement that incorporated provisions similar to those described in Martin's letter.[51]

The dismissals triggered a bitter dispute between GM and the UAW. That same Wednesday, the Pontiac local's newspaper denounced the firings as indicative of "lawless company agression" and accused the corporation of provoking wildcats by its insistence on a "terrific speed-up and wholesale sabotaging of the union agreement."[52]

At 3:30 on the same day, Wednesday, November 17, 500 workers again occupied the Fisher Body Plant. Those inside the plant welded one of the gates shut and moved in blankets and food stores. This time the Pontiac workers were ready for a long siege.[53]

At first, the Communist party supported the Pontiac occupation. In its first article on the Wednesday strike, the *Daily Worker* sympathetically quoted Method's comment that the Pontiac workers had been forced "to take the measure they deemed best" in order to defend the four fired leaders who "they rightly felt had been unjustly treated."[54]

The first official union response was not entirely negative either. William Munger, UAW research director and a Lovestoneite, blamed the second sit-down on management's "failure to negotiate satisfactorily." Richard Frankensteen, second only to Martin in the UAW hierarchy, also indicated his sympathy with the strike. "It is my belief that General Motors could have prevented all of this trouble by offering the union a sufficiently decent contract."[55]

The union's official stance changed rapidly and dramatically. On Thursday, the day after the strike had begun, Martin again denounced wildcats and urged the Pontiac strikers to return to work. That evening a meeting of 2,500 Pontiac workers heard Fred Pieper, a Martin supporter on the union executive board, press for an immediate evacuation of the plant. Those in attendance voted overwhelmingly to continue the strike.[56]

Morale among the Pontiac workers remained at a very high level throughout the first days of the strike, despite police harrassment and pressure from the union's officialdom. At all times, day and night, 200 people remained in the plant. More than 500 workers were directly involved in the sit-down, with most of them taking revolving shifts inside the plant.[57]

On Saturday evening, four days into the strike, the Pontiac Fisher Body workers hosted a dance inside the factory. Hundreds of auto workers in the Detroit area showed their support for the sit-down by taking their dates to the dance. The plant was guarded by men with fire hoses to ensure that the festivities were not disturbed.[58]

The resolve of the Pontiac strikers created an acute crisis for the UAW leadership. Homer Martin was perfectly aware that GM would refuse to negotiate with the UAW until the union hierarchy demonstrated its ability to police the ranks. General Motors made this very clear in its first official response to the Pontiac occupation. William Knudsen, GM president, publicly demanded that the UAW bring the strike to an immediate end. In a statement issued on Friday, November 19, he insisted that unauthorized strikes such as that in Pontiac "will eventually make agreements valueless and collective bargaining impossible in practice."[59]

Knudsen's threatening letter was not the only pressure being brought to bear on the UAW leadership. Michigan's governor, Frank Murphy, who had campaigned with CIO endorsement, threatened to send in the militia to clear the plant of strikers so production could be speedily resumed. In addition, John L. Lewis told Martin and the UAW leadership that he would insist on a quick end to all wildcat strikes. A showdown at Pontiac was imminent.[60]

Martin knew that his credibility as a "responsible" union official depended on his success in quickly ending the Pontiac strike. He therefore convoked an emergency meeting of the union's executive board for Sunday morning, November 21, in Detroit. The conflict came to a head at this climactic meeting. George Method, the chief sparkplug of the strike, was summoned to Detroit to report to the executive officers. Method defended the strike and cited GM's intransigence in settling local grievances as the key factor provoking the dispute. Method also reaffirmed the demands of the strikers to the UAW hierarchy. The Pontiac plant would only be evacuated when the four fired leaders, including himself, were rehired, when GM committed itself to reversing its decision to shift work from Pontiac to Linden, New Jersey, and when the corporation agreed to rehire the Fisher Body Plant's laid-off workers.[61]

The executive board split sharply in its reaction to Method's presentation and to the Pontiac occupation. Both Mortimer and Reuther urged the board to authorize the strike officially, so no one else would be victimized by management. Under their plan, the union would then call for the immediate evacuation of the plant so that the dismissal of the four local leaders could be reversed through negotiations.

Martin rejected the Mortimer–Reuther proposal and instead pressed the board to demand an unconditional end to the strike. After several hours of heated debate, the executive board temporarily adjourned, having been unable to reach a clear-cut decision. Another session was set for late that night in Pontiac, 25 miles from Detroit.[62]

Martin then went to Pontiac to address a rally of 1,500 workers. There he again condemned the strike and insisted that unauthorized strikes "will ruin the union." Martin's speech set off a heated debate that ended in another vote by the Pontiac workers to continue the strike.[63]

A small-scale wildcat at Pontiac Fisher Body had thus sparked a major crisis within the UAW. From Method to Mortimer, Communists had been instrumental in the strike, at the shop-floor to the union's executive board. Yet within a 24-hour period, the CP reversed its stance of qualified support and used its authority to implement an immediate end to the strike.

Late Sunday night, the board resumed its emergency meeting in Pontiac. Mortimer and Reuther continued to advocate their plan as a workable compromise, but this time Martin had the votes to pass a resolution denying official authorization to the strike. Still the union's leaders had to figure out how to enforce their evacuation order before the state militia was sent into action and a bloody battle ensued.[64]

Martin succeeded in accomplishing this by leaking his version of the events to Louis Stark, the labor reporter of the *New York Times*. In an

article bylined Sunday, November 21, Stark wrote that the Martin administration "believes that its union opponents wish to foment
unauthorized strikes in order to cast discredit on the chief leaders." According to Stark, Martin was "under pressure from both communist party
leadership and from militant socialists."[65]

This article was a bombshell. The CP was being blamed for instigating
a major confrontation in the auto industry at the same time as it was
desperately seeking to project itself as a legitimate component of the New
Deal coalition.

Within hours after the *New York Times* had published the article, the
CP had ordered an end to the occupation. Earl Browder personally intervened to order the party's auto faction to bring about an immediate halt
to the sit-down.[66] By Monday morning, the cadre had been told of this
switch in line and had adjusted their position accordingly.

When the executive board adjourned in the early hours of Monday
morning, after an all-night session, it had finally decided to call for an unconditional end to the strike. Yet the workers inside the plant continued to
stand firm and the stalemate continued. Martin went to sleep early Monday
morning, only to be awakened and told a couple of hours later that the sit-
downers were now prepared to hear him. At 10:30 A.M., Martin went into
the plant and ordered the men to leave immediately. His order to evacuate
was seconded by George Method, until then the unofficial leader of the
strike. Method told the workers, "We are all wrong. Let's go out of the
plant and show we are behind the international union." At 11:30 A.M.,
Monday, November 22, the strikers left the plant, and the Pontiac occupation was over. The defeat was total, the four local leaders stayed fired, and
the local union was soon placed under trusteeship.[67]

The CP quickly distanced itself from the Pontiac sit-down. On the
same day the strike ended, Martin received a message from party head-
quarters in New York that, according to Stark, declared "that the
Communists were '100 per cent' with him in his handling of the Pontiac
situation." Mortimer told a rally of Pontiac workers the same afternoon
that the UAW board's decision "must be abided by" and, further, that
"the Board was unanimous in its oppositon" to wildcats.[68]

For the Communist party, Pontiac had been a dangerous gamble, one
that had nearly led to a disastrous setback for its Popular Front strategy.
The top echelon had been drawn into an impasse over a local union dispute.
For the party, the lesson was clear. Once the strike was over, the CP
staunchly insisted that it had never condoned the Pontiac strike and that it
abhorred all wildcats, past or future. A few days after the end of the strike,
a *Daily Worker* editorial argued that wildcats "only play into the hands of
General Motors."[69] A leading party functionary, William Weinstone, also
wrote that "the Communists and the Communist Party have never in the

past, and do not now, in any shape, manner or form advocate or support unauthorized and wildcat actions.''

The party was quite explicit about the rationale for this policy statement. Popular Front policies were designed to legitimate the CP as a responsible and respected component of the New Deal coalition. For Weinstone, to be seen as the initiators of militant actions could only be "gravely injurious . . . to the cause of cooperative action between labor and middle-class groups."[70] The CP thus reversed its initial hesitant support for the Pontiac sit-down and reverted to a position of vehement opposition to unauthorized strikes.

THE FINAL BREAK

The strike at the Pontiac Fisher Body Plant marked a high point in rank and file militancy during the first formative years of the UAW. Soon afterward, shop-floor morale was undermined by massive lay-offs as auto sales went into a severe slump. By January 1938, over one-quarter of GM's production workers were laid off, and the proportion was considerably higher for the other auto corporations.[71] For the next months, internal conflicts within the UAW centered on controversial issues within the wider society, while clashes with GM receded in significance.

Immediately after the Pontiac strike, the CP became far friendlier toward Homer Martin. It had discovered the hard way that opposition to Martin's policies was likely to lead its cadre to support more militant tactics, tactics that the party believed were inconsistent with its Popular Front strategy. The alternative was to win Martin away from his alliance with the Lovestoneites.

The *Daily Worker* sympathetically reported Martin's activities in the weeks following the Pontiac strike. In particular, Martin was lauded for sending "a wire to Roosevelt in which he [Martin] praised his message to Congress and assured him of the support of the union for all of the policies outlined in the address."[72]

Within the UAW, the Communist forces backed Martin's drive to suppress any signs of militancy. Soon after the Pontiac strike, the CP's leaders informed Martin that its cadre would support his moves to shut all local newspapers. This was primarily aimed at Reuther's *West Side Conveyor*, a focal point for opposition forces in the union. At is January 1938 meeting, Communist sympathizers on the UAW executive board voted to reaffirm Martin's September letter to GM, again conceding to the corporation total control over workplace discipline as a prerequisite to the resumption of negotiations for a new contract.[73]

Ironically, as the CP sought to mollify Martin, he broke with it on a vital foreign policy question, the Ludlow Amendment, and thus precipitated the final split in relations. This split can only be understood in the context of party policy as it evolved after Roosevelt's " 'quarantine', the aggressors" speech of October 1937.

From mid-1936 until Roosevelt's speech, the CP had sought to become an influential element of the progressive wing of New Deal supporters, hoping that FDR would have to respond to these forces and not just to the conservatives within the Democratic party. In his "quarantine" speech, Roosevelt clearly signaled his willingness to enter into a global alliance with the Soviet Union in opposition to the fascist powers.[74] For the Communist party, the top priority became directly building support for Roosevelt, particularly for his policy of moving the United States toward alliances for "collective security."[75]

The CP was therefore dismayed by one item on the January 1938 executive board agenda. Homer Martin came out for the Ludlow Amendment and carried the board with him. The amendment would have placed into the U.S. Constitution a mandate that a declaration of war could only go into effect by a majority vote in a national referendum.[76]

Although the specific wording of the amendment permitted the president to bypass the referendum in case of a direct attack, the CP was horrified by the proposal and bitterly attacked its supporters. As early as December 1937, the *Daily Worker* insisted that passage of the amendment would "not serve the cause of peace, because the net result is to put obstacles in the path of cooperative action of the U.S. with other nations to insure world peace."[77]

The Communist party was the only group on the Left to denounce the Ludlow Amendment. The Socialist party strongly opposed U.S. war preparations, and it viewed the amendment as one step in its overall campaign to resist U.S. participation in a global war. A week after the *Daily Worker* editorial, the *Socialist Call*, the official SP newspaper, reported that "the Communist Party has become one of the most aggressive forces in America advancing the imperialist policies of the American reactionaries."[78]

From the time of the Communist party's decision to support the New Deal coalition in mid-1936, relations between CP and SP activists in the auto industry had been strained, but this dispute was different. Antiwar sentiment was widespread, and the Ludlow Amendment had enormous popularity.[79] This made it easier for Socialist activists to argue for the amendment within the union, and they proceeded to do just that.

The conflict still would not have come to a head without the intervention of the Lovestoneites. One week before the January 1938 executive board meeting, the Lovestone paper, *Workers Age*, declared its support for the Ludlow Amendment, arguing that agitation for its passage "would offer at least the possibility of raising our voice against predatory wars of American imperialism."[80]

Lovestone's supporters in the UAW were able to convince Martin to present support for Ludlow as a keystone of his administration. The executive board resolution gave "wholehearted endorsement" to the Ludlow Amendment and went further to demand that "the foreign policy of the U.S. shall not be formulated or made dependent upon the protection of the vested or property interests in foreign countries of the large corporations in this country." Martin also denounced Roosevelt in the UAW newspaper for war-mongering and reiterated "that it is important and necessary that the LaFollette–Ludlow Amendment become a part of the Constitution."[81]

The crisis over the Ludlow Amendment led to the final break in relations between the CP and Martin. The party had desperately sought to avoid a clash with the UAW president after Pontiac, but on the most sensitive of subjects, the creation of a global antifascist alliance, Martin had rejected the party line and attacked Roosevelt. This time the split was final, and the battle was fought to the bitter end.

Soon after the UAW board meeting, the *Daily Worker* shrilly attacked the Lovestoneite support for Ludlow, arguing that this gave "assistance to the Fascist enemies of America's participation in collective peace action." Yet open warfare with Martin only erupted two weeks later when Martin again denounced the CP to the *New York Times* and reaffirmed his determination to drive the Communists out of the union. In a page one editorial, the *Daily Worker* declared that the CP would not allow Martin to purge its cadres and that the party would actively organize against his administration. The editorial also denounced Martin's support for Ludlow as symptomatic of the Lovestoneite influence in the UAW.[82]

More authoritative denunciations followed. Communist party chairman William Z. Foster wrote a detailed analysis of the reasons for the split with Martin. A key point was the UAW executive board resolution on the Ludlow Amendment, which Foster cited as a "surrender to fascism." Earl Browder, on returning from a trip to Europe, criticized Martin for his "isolationist shouting," and because he "openly demands complete acceptance of the demands of Japanese imperialism by the United States government." Homer Martin had been excommunicated.[83]

With its efforts at developing an alliance with Martin at an end, the CP quickly sought out a new ally. Richard Frankensteen was ambitious and opportunistic. He was also an avid supporter of Roosevelt and a fervent backer of the administration's "collective security" program.

In early 1938, three key CP leaders, Foster, Weinstone, and Gebert, met secretly with Frankensteen to work out a cooperative arrangement. In return for splitting with Martin, Frankensteen was promised the party's endorsement and aid in his future campaign for higher office. The deal was struck, and Frankensteen was soon denouncing factional disputes and distancing himself from the incumbent administration. Soon news of the secret meeting became public, but the arrangement held. The CP had successfully forged an alliance with the most politically moderate member of the UAW leadership.[84]

As this deal unfolded, the CP began to break openly with Reuther and the UAW's Socialist party activists. By the fall of 1937, relations between the CP and Walter Reuther had already become strained. Reuther's active participation in the drive to defeat the November tentative contract contrasted markedly with the more cautious approach of the party. The Pontiac sit-down exacerbated the tensions, particularly when the CP abruptly reversed its position to call for an unconditional end to the strike.

Nevertheless, as with its relationship to Martin, it was the Ludlow Amendment that first precipitated an open breach between the CP and Reuther. Reuther voted for the executive board resolution on Ludlow, and he then backed up this position by publicly endorsing nationwide demonstrations called for March 1938 to support the Ludlow Amendment and to protest the drift toward war. In addition, Local 174, Reuther's home base and a center of Socialist party influence in the UAW, sent delegates to a national antiwar conference over the heated opposition of the small CP opposition in the local.[85]

To the Communist party, these actions constituted an unforgiveable affront, and it quickly moved to retaliate. The Unity caucus, CP and SP, had agreed to support Victor Reuther for secretary-treasurer of the Michigan CIO at its April 1938 meeting. Later, after the conference was already in session, the CP decided to renege on this arrangement, in part as a favor to Frankensteen, who was backing another candidate. Victor Reuther was defeated, and relations with the Reuthers nearly came to an open split. The party afterward defended its move by arguing that the SP played a factional role in the UAW, and because of this, the election of Victor Reuther, then still a SP member, would be "endangering the organizational unity not only of the auto workers, but of other unionists as well."[86]

By April 1938, the CP was locked into a pitched battle with Homer Martin at the same time as its relationship with Walter Reuther was rapidly deteriorating. As it happened, the tactical need to maintain a united front against Martin's frontal assault forced the CP and the Reuther–SP forces to remain in an uneasy coalition over the next year of internecine warfare. When the smoke had cleared and the UAW had reconstituted itself without Martin, the factional dispute between the CP and Reuther again became the crucial one in the union. The Communists maintained their alliance with Frankensteen, thus broadening their coalition to include some of the more conservative elements in the UAW leadership. By the 1940 convention, Reuther had forged his own unsavory alliance, in his case with the Association of Catholic Trade Unionists (ACTU), an explicitly anticommunist grouping backed by the Catholic church.[87]

A SUMMING UP

Throughout World War II, the two caucuses remained roughly even in influence, with neither one in a position to crush the other one. This stalemate ended after the war, when Reuther was able to use the anticommunist hysteria of the postwar period to undercut Communist support in the UAW.

The opportunistic maneuvering of the Communist party, its willingness to sacrifice rank and file militancy in order to further its strategic goals, and its own unprincipled deals with careerist officials such as Frankensteen eroded its support among the radicalized activists who were the core of the early UAW. The erosion became even more acute during World War II, when the party initiated a drive to institute incentive pay plans in UAW plants and it avidly defended the no-strike pledge. In the long-run, the CP's drive to gain respectability, both during the late 1930s and during World War II, only made it more vulnerable to attack when the Cold War began.

Far more importantly, Popular Front politics provided one more roadblock to the continued development of a self-aware and militant working class. As we have seen through an analysis of the UAW from 1936 to 1938, the Popular Front had implications for party strategy in every arena, and in particular for its trade union work. For UAW militants, the implications were disastrous, as the CP consistently denounced wildcats, while it fruitlessly sought an alliance with the inept and timid Homer Martin.

Stripped of its radical rhetoric, CP policy in the UAW was hesitant and cautious at a time when the militancy of the rank and file demanded boldness and audacity. The party thereby contributed substantially to the establishment of a pattern of management–labor relations in which the union limited its efforts to gain higher wages and benefits for its members, while the corporations retained their tight control over the production process.

Breaking out of this pattern would have been difficult to achieve in any case. Without the active support of CP cadre in the auto industry, it proved to be impossible.

NOTES

1. Bert Cochran, *Labor and Communism* (Princeton, New Jersey: Princeton University Press), pp. 44–66. As late as April 1934, Earl Browder, CP general secretary, argued that "fascism must find indirect support. This it finds in the Socialist Party and the reformist trade union officialdom." Earl Browder, *Communism in the United States* (New York: International Publishers, 1935), p. 28.

2. Roger Keeran, *The Communist Party and the Auto Worker* (Bloomington, Indiana: Indiana University Press, 1980), pp. 33–59.

3. Cochran, *Labor and Communism*, p. 75.

4. Walter Galenson, *The CIO Challenge to the AFL* (Cambridge, Massachusetts: Harvard University Press, 1960), pp. 124–27.

5. Cochran, *Labor and Communism*, p. 57.

6. Frank Marquart, *An Auto Worker's Journal* (University Park, Pennsylvania: Pennsylvania State University Press, 1975), pp. 80–82; Irving Howe and B. J. Widick, *The UAW and Walter Reuther* (New York: Random House, 1949), p. 195.

7. Howe and Widick, *UAW and Walter Reuther*, pp. 189–93; Frank Cormier and William J. Eaton, *Reuther* (Englewood Cliffs, New Jersey: Prentice-Hall, 1970), pp. 1–46.

8. Galenson, *CIO Challenge*, pp. 131, 152.

9. UAW-CIO, *Proceedings of the Second Annual Convention* (South Bend, Indiana: May 1936), p. 163.

10. Ibid, p. 253.

11. Ibid, p. 265; *Socialist Call*, May 9, 1936; Howe and Widick, *UAW and Walter Reuther*, p. 53.

12. Earl Browder, "The Communists in the People's Front," *Communist* 16 (July 1937): 610.

13. Keeran, *Communist Party*, pp. 148–85. For a description of the Flint sit-down and the agreement that ended it see Galenson, *CIO Challenge*, pp. 135–41.

14. Galenson, *CIO Challenge*, pp. 148–49.

15. Browder, "Communists in the People's Front," p. 610.

16. Ibid, p. 610.

17. A description of the shop steward system by William Munger is in *Workers Age*, March 5, 1938. Munger was UAW Research Director and a Lovestoneite.

18. *United Automobile Worker*, March 12, 1938; April 9, 1938.

19. *United Automobile Worker*, May 22, 1937; April 9, 1938; Report of Elmer Dowell to UAW Executive Board, May 11, 1938, George Addes Papers, Box 9, Walter P. Reuther Library, Wayne State University, Detroit, Michigan.

20. *United Automobile Worker*, June 19, 1937.

21. *New York Times*, July 21, 1937.

22. *New York Times*, June 19, 1937.

23. *New York Times*, June 19, 1937.

24. *New York Times*, September 17, 1937. The UAW reported that there had been no wildcats in GM plants during the previous three months. This held true until the rejection of the tentative contract in mid-November and the Pontiac strike.

25. *New York Times*, June 30, 1937.

26. Earl Browder, *The People's Front* (New York: International Publishers, 1938), p. 63.

27. Wyndham Mortimer and Ed Hall, Press Release, August 7, 1937, Henry Kraus Papers, Walter P. Reuther Library, Wayne State University, Detroit, Michigan; *Daily Worker*, July 19, 1937.

28. Galenson, *CIO Challenge*, p. 153.

29. Theodore Draper, *American Communism and Soviet Russia* (New York: Viking, 1960), pp. 377–430; Cochran, *Labor and Communism*, pp. 131–33.

30. Galenson, *CIO Challenge*, p. 153.

31. Keeran, *Communist Party*, pp. 191–92.

32. B. K. Gebert, *Daily Worker*, July 22, 1937; Victor Reuther, *The Brothers Reuther* (Boston: Houghton Mifflin, 1979), p. 186.

33. UAW-CIO, *Proceedings of the Third Annual Convention* (Milwaukee, Wisconsin, 1937), pp. 53, 228. Local 155 was chartered by the UAW in 1935, but it had been organized earlier as part of an independent union of skilled workers (MESA). When the CP decided to go

into the AFL, the party took its base in the small tool and die shops into the UAW as Local 155. Cochran, *Labor and Communism*, p. 70.

34. Cochran, *Labor and Communism*, p. 156; Galenson, *CIO Challenge*, p. 153; *New York Times*, November 27, 1937.

35. B. K. Gebert, "The Convention of 400,000," *Communist* 16 (October 1937): 894, 901, 904.

36. Galenson, *CIO Challenge*, p. 159; *New York Times*, November 28, 1937.

37. *Daily Worker*, October 5, 1937.

38. *United Automobile Worker*, September 18, 1937. On July 20, 1937, Knudsen had sent a letter to the UAW demanding that the union accept the following contract provision as a prerequisite to further negotiations: in regard to unauthorized strikes, the corporation "shall forthwith discharge the employee or employees guilty thereof, and the union shall take suitable disciplinary action against the parties responsible." *New York Times*, July 21, 1937. Martin's letter represented a total acquiescence to GM's demand.

39. *West Side Conveyor*, November 16, 1937.

40. William Weinstone, "The Great Auto Strike," *Communist* 16 (March 1937): 226-27.

41. *Socialist Call*, August 7, 1937.

42. Cochran, *Labor and Communism*, p. 110; Keeran, *Communist Party*, p. 157.

43. Marquart, *Auto Workers Journal*, p. 81.

44. *West Side Conveyor*, November 9, 1937; November 16, 1937.

45. *Detroit Free Press*, November 13, 1937; *West Side Conveyor*, November 16, 1937.

46. UAW-CIO, Proceedings of the GM Delegates Conference, Detroit, November 1937, Fred Pieper Collection, Walter P. Reuther Library, Wayne State University, Detroit, Michigan.

47. *New York Times*, November 16, 1937; *Detroit News*, November 18, 1937; November 20, 1937.

48. *Detroit Free Press*, November 17, 1937; *Pontiac Auto Worker* (Local 159), November 17, 1937.

49. UAW-CIO, Proceedings of the GM Delegates Conference.

50. *New York Times*, November 15, 1937; November 16, 1937; *Detroit News*, November 16, 1937.

51. *New York Times*, November 18, 1937; *Detroit News*, November 18, 1937.

52. *Pontiac Auto Worker* (Local 159), November 17, 1937.

53. *Detroit News*, November 18, 1937; *New York Times*, November 19, 1937.

54. *Daily Worker*, November 20, 1937. Lawrence Emery, the *Daily Worker*'s labor reporter, had written a previous sympathetic report on the first quickie strike in Pontiac, holding that it "compelled the management to negotiate" over plant lay-offs. *Daily Worker*, November 18, 1937.

55. *New York Times*, November 18, 1937; *Daily News*, November 19, 1937.

56. *New York Times*, November 29, 1937; *Detroit News*, November 19, 1937.

57. *Detroit Free Press*, November 22, 1937.

58. *Detroit Free Press*, November 22, 1937; *New York Times*, November 21, 1937.

59. *New York Times*, November 20, 1937.

60. *New York Times*, November 22, 1937.

61. *New York Times*, November 21, 1937; November 22, 1937; *Detroit Free Press*, November 22, 1937. The most detailed listing of the strikers' demands is in the *Detroit Free Press*, November 20, 1937.

62. *New York Times*, November 23, 1937; *Detroit Free Press*, November 22, 1937.

63. *Detroit Free Press*, November 22, 1937.

64. *New York Times*, November 23, 1937; *Detroit Free Press*, November 22, 1937.

65. *New York Times*, November 22, 1937.

66. *Daily Worker*, November 23, 1937. It is difficult to pinpoint the exact time of Browder's intervention. The *Daily Worker* reported that he intervened on Tuesday, November

23, after the strike had ended and when the party was eager to demonstrate its role in opposing all wildcats, past and future. There is every reason to believe that Browder personally ordered an end to the strike, but the *Daily Worker* editorial places the time of Browder's meeting with the relevant party functionaries on Friday, November 19. This is certainly too early.

First, Stark's article blaming the CP for instigating the strike did not appear until the Monday, November 22 edition. Further, we know that as of Sunday afternoon Method was still defending the strike to the union executive board, and Mortimer was still giving qualified support to the strikers. If Browder told the cadre to end the strike on Friday, internal communications within the CP must have been very slow indeed.

It is far more likely that the Browder meeting took place late Sunday night or very early Monday morning, when Stark's article would have been available in New York, and that the *Daily Worker* conveniently pushed back the date to Friday, in order to present the misleading impression that the party had consistently and virtually from the start opposed the Pontiac strike. In any case, by Monday morning the party line had shifted.

67. *New York Times*, November 23, 1937; *Detroit Free Press*, November 22, 1937; *New York Times*, November 29, 1937.

68. *New York Times*, November 24, 1937; *Pontiac Auto Worker* (Local 159), November 24, 1937.

69. *Daily Worker*, November 23, 1937.

70. *Daily Worker*, December 2, 1937.

71. *Daily Worker*, January 8, 1938. The data is from Martin's testimony to a Senate hearing on unemployment. Production fell precipitously after Christmas, 1937. United States car production dropped from 295,000 in November 1937 to 155,000 in January 1938, with most of the decline coming in late December and early January. Ward's Communications, *Ward's Automotive Year Book* (Detroit: 1938), pp. 10–11. Employment fell from 517,000 in 1937 to 305,000 in 1938 for the entire industry. Ward's Communications, *Ward's Automotive Year Book* (Detroit: 1943), p. 27.

72. *Daily Worker*, January 10, 1938.

73. *New York Times*, November 27, 1937; *Daily Worker*, January 18, 1938.

74. Franklin D. Roosevelt, "The Will for Peace," in *Nothing to Fear, Selected Addresses* ed. B. D. Zevin (Cambridge, Massachusetts: Houghton, Mifflin, 1946), pp. 110–15.

75. During this period, the party called for the formation of a "Democratic Front" to include the working class, the middle class and the farmers under the banner of the New Deal. Earl Browder held that "this New Deal wing under Roosevelt is an essential part of the developing democratic front against monopoly capital." Earl Browder, *The Democratic Front* (New York: Workers Library, 1938), p. 16. This is from a speech to the May 1938 CP convention.

76. The amendment became a vital issue in December 1937, when its supporters got it out of committee and onto the House floor. Roosevelt used all of his resources as President to squelch it, and, at the end of January 1938, the amendment was defeated by a narrow vote in the House of Representatives. William E. Leuchtenburg, *Franklin D. Roosevelt and the New Deal, 1932–49* (New York: Harper and Row, 1963), pp. 228–30.

77. *Daily Worker*, December 18, 1937.

78. *Socialist Call*, December 25, 1937.

79. Seventy-three percent of those polled supported the essence of the Ludlow Amendment in September 1937. George Gallup, *The Gallup Polls, 1935–71* (New York: Random House, 1972), 1: 71.

80. *Workers Age*, January 8, 1938.

81. *United Automobile Worker*, January 22, 1938; January 15, 1938.

82. *New York Times*, February 4, 1938; *Daily Worker*, February 5, 1938.

83. *Daily Worker*, March 28, 1938; Earl Browder, *Concerted Action or Isolation* (New York: Workers Library, 1938), p. 46.

84. Galenson, *CIO Challenge*, pp. 159–60. Rumors as to Frankensteen's aspirations differed as to specifics. Frankensteen may have wanted to become UAW president, but he was also interested in Democratic party politics, and the Socialist party believed he was intent on running for lieutenant governor. *Socialist Call*, May 7, 1938.

85. *Socialist Call*, May 21, 1938; *Workers Age*, March 5, 1938.

86. Clayton Fountain, *Union Guy* (New York: Viking Press, 1949), pp. 83–85; William Weinstone and B. K. Gebert, *Daily Worker*, May 10, 1938.

87. Cochran, *Labor and Communism*, p. 152.

PART III
THE SHACHTMAN
TENDENCY

Although the Communist party was the dominant force on the Left during the 1930s, it had influential rivals. The twists and turns of Comintern policy led to frequent splits, with a concomitant proliferation of organizations. Most of these splinter parties vanished quickly, leaving little in their wake. One important exception was the Trotskyist tendency, which continues to have an organizational presence and which has had a considerable impact on the ideological development of the U.S. Left.

My focus will not be on the orthodox Trotskyism of the Socialist Workers party, but instead I will highlight third camp socialism, a significant offshoot of Trotskyism. This tendency rejected Trotsky's critical defense of the Soviet Union as a degenerated workers state and instead argued that the Soviet Union was a new type of exploitative class society. In its organizational form of the 1940s and 1950s, third camp socialism remained a small and powerless sect, but it still provided the lively training ground for many contemporary socialists, including such influential ideologues, writers, and activists as Michael Harrington and Irving Howe.

The historical roots of third camp politics can be found in the first formative years of U.S. Trotskyism.

8
THE TROTSKYISTS DURING THE 1930s

Trotskyism in the United States was very much the product of the U.S. Communist party. When James P. Cannon and his less than 100 followers were expelled from the CP in October 1928,[1] their first response was to view themselves as the "true Communists" who adhered to a genuinely Leninist perspective. Even after they formed their own organization, the Trotskyists still insisted that they remained loyal members of the CP but that their expulsions from the CP temporarily prevented them from directly participating in it. The new organization was intended as a strictly temporary measure, a pressure group that would influence CP policies from the outside until the course of events compelled the readmission of the Trotskyists into the CP.[2]

From the start, U.S. Trotskyists advocated an electoral policy similar to that previously articulated by the Communist party. The CP had been urging the formation of a broadly based labor party, and indeed it had even supported a right-wing member of the Socialist party on an independent ticket for municipal judge in New York City.[3] In early 1928, Cannon had been approached by Maurice Spector, a leading figure in the Canadian CP and a secret sympathizer of Trotsky's. Spector informed Cannon of Trotsky's critique of Stalin, which Cannon had only known before in a grossly distorted form. As it happened, Cannon's final conversion to Trotskyism took place at the Sixth Comintern Congress, the meeting at which the Comintern officially sanctioned the belief in the Third Period of capitalist collapse and world revolution.[4]

From this point until late in 1934, the Communist party totally rejected support for a labor party and insisted instead that the CP itself was "the only way out" of the growing economic crisis. Cannon and his fellow Trotskyists rejected the CP's ultra-leftist rhetoric and continued to call for broadly based independent political action, in keeping with the Communist party's previous policy.

The Trotskyist position on electoral policy was most clearly articulated by Max Shachtman, the new organization's leading ideologue. Shachtman was first attracted to socialist politics in high school, when he enrolled in the SP youth group. Buoyed by enthusiasm for the Russian Revolution, he joined one of the SP's left-wing splinter groups, the Workers Council. In 1922, this group was absorbed by the Communist party, and Shachtman became a leader of the Communist youth section. He aligned himself with Cannon in the CP's internal disputes, and he was then expelled with Cannon in 1928 for Trotskyist deviations.[5] In one of the first issues of the new organization's paper, *The Militant*, Shachtman wrote that he saw "no reason to put aside the perspective of a labor party development in the working class movement."[6]

At its 1929 founding convention, the new Trotskyist organization, the Communist League of America (CLA), included in its platform a statement of support for a labor party. The CLA reaffirmed its belief that "the perspective of a Labor Party as a primary development of the American workers . . . .holds good today." Furthermore, the platform continued, "it is not reasonable to expect that the masses of American workers, who are still tied ideologically and politically to the bourgeois parties will come over to the Communist Party politically at one step in a period not immediately revolutionary."[7]

The Trotskyist position, which directly challenged the Third Period politics of the CP, was deeply rooted in Marxist tradition. The Trotskyists specifically cited as support for their position a 1922 directive from the Comintern to the Communist party, which urged the party to promote the formation of a broadly based labor party.[8] Yet the CLA platform strictly limited its support to a labor party organized on the basis of bloc voting by the trade unions, rather than on individual memberships. Such a structure, modeled on the British Labor party, would ensure working class control of the new party and would prevent its capture by petit-bourgeois elements, such as small farmers or middle-class professionals.[9]

At the time of the 1928 expulsions of his supporters from the U.S. CP, Trotsky was still in exile in Siberia. Soon afterward, he was allowed to emigrate from the Soviet Union and to move to Prinkipo, Turkey. From 1930 on, the leaders of the Trotskyist tendency were in constant contact with their leader, who, in turn, increasingly involved himself in the internal life of the new party.

By this time, the CP had moved firmly into the Third Period phase and was busy denouncing the idea of a labor party as a reformist illusion. In early 1930, when Shachtman arrived in Prinkipo as the first envoy of U.S. Trotskyism, Trotsky was quick to suggest a new perspective for the CLA. There was no reason to believe "that the American workers will perforce have to pass through the school of reformism." In particular, "the stage of the labor party . . . is by no means inevitable." The deepening economic crisis created a situation in which "a combination of forces is possible . . . [such that] the tempo of development in the United States is enormously accelerated."[10]

On the basis of this rather sketchy analysis, the Trotskyist tendency in this country reversed the position it had held on independent political action for more than seven years. In a 1931 resolution, the CLA, acting in its role as CP gadfly, declared that the "American Communists cannot undertake to organize a petty bourgeois party standing between the bourgeoisie and the proletariat." Instead, the Trotskyists urged the CP in the 1932 elections to "enter that campaign under their own banner and in direct struggle against their reformist antagonists, the Socialist party."[11]

The choice, either capitalist reaction or socialist revolution, was stark, and a labor party could only confuse the working class from clearly seeing this basic choice. The Trotskyist position was thus almost identical to that of the Communist party during its Third Period phase, only without the "social fascist" rhetoric.

Trotsky publicly supported the new line from his exile in Prinkipo. The need for independent political action was "a commonplace for a Marxist," and this included an understanding "that the inevitable and imminent development of a party of the working class will totally change the political face of the United States." Yet the U.S. trade union bureaucracy was so conservative that "the creation of a labor party could be provoked only by a mighty revolutionary pressure from the working masses and by the growing threat of communism." But "under these conditions the labor party would signify not a progressive step but a hindrance."

Trotsky further argued that if a labor party were formed, revolutionaries would have to participate in it but "only under the condition that we consider the labor party not as 'our' party, but as an arena in which we are acting as an absolutely independent Communist party." While entry into a genuine labor party was possible, this was out of the question for a farmer–labor party. In Trotsky's view, "the idea of a farmer–labor party is a treacherous mockery of Marxism."[12]

The 1931 platform remained the basis for the Trotskyist perspective on independent political action until 1938. Indeed, in 1935, when the Communist party line shifted to support for a nation-wide farmer labor party, Shachtman harshly criticized the Communists for this reversal. He argued that it was not "the business of the revolutionary Marxists, above all in the present stage of the relationship between capitalist disintegration and social reformism, to initiate or to help organize" a labor party.

Shachtman went on to present the most cogent set of arguments for opposing the formation of a labor party by anyone within the Trotskyist tradition. He held that the existing economic crisis eliminated the possibility of a viable, reformist working class party. The British Labour party could be successfully started at the turn of the century because capitalism still had a certain vitality, and thus working class pressure could still wring significant concessions from the capitalist class. By the 1930s and the advent of the Great Depression, this situation no longer held. While Marxists had always called for the formation of an independent party of the working class, this was "obsolete advice" and to follow it would be "to ignore the tremendous changes that have taken place." As the economic crisis deepened, the working class would rapidly become radicalized and might even "skip 'stages' with even greater ease and speed than their Russian brothers." With the onset of the permanent crisis of capitalism, "the only genuine labor party is the party of revolutionary Marxism."

As in the 1931 platform, Shachtman did not entirely rule out the possibility of a mass labor party being formed, but it would be formed by the trade union bureaucracy "for the express purpose of thwarting the working class." For this reason, such a party would be "a directly anti-revolutionary (ergo anti-progressive) party." Nonetheless, should a labor party be formed, the Trotskyists would enter it, but only as a disciplined faction hostile to its reformist leadership.[13]

When the Trotskyists dissolved into the Socialist party in 1936, the Trotskyist position on electoral activity remained unchanged. In fact, one of the most bitter disputes within the unified SP centered on its attitude toward the farmer–labor parties of Minnesota and Wisconsin. The majority of the SP was in favor of entering these formations, while maintaining the right to a separate organizational existence as one component of a broader alliance. The Trotskyist opposition sharply attacked this position as opportunistic and urged the SP to present itself instead as the nucleus of a mass, revolutionary party.[14]

The faction fight within the SP was vitriolic and destructive, but it was also short-lived. By late 1937, the Trotskyist tendency had been expelled from the Socialist party, and, by early 1938, U.S. Trotskyism again had its own organization, the Socialist Workers party (SWP).[15]

Soon the new party found itself in the midst of its own internal struggle over the same issue, the correct attitude to adopt toward the farmer–labor party. The Minnesota SWP members were central to this internal struggle since they had become leading officials in Teamsters Local 544, then a dynamic force for industrial unionism throughout the region. As leaders of the Minneapolis trade union movement, they found it necessary to relate to the farmer–labor party.

The Minnesota Farmer–Labor party (FLP) had been formed in 1918 as a coalition of activist farmers organized into the Non-Partisan League and the state's progressive unions. The party was the only one of its kind to survive the debacle of LaFollette's 1924 presidential campaign, but it only became a serious electoral force with the advent of the Great Depression. By 1936, the FLP was Minnesota's majority party, having elected the governor, both U.S. Senators, five out of nine Congresspeople, and a majority of the state Representatives.[16]

Given the size and importance of the Minnesota Farmer–Labor party, there were enormous pressures on the Minneapolis Teamsters to participate actively in that broadly based party. Trotsky had allowed the Teamster comrades a certain freedom from party orthodoxy, so that in 1935 the Local 544 paper could tepidly support Thomas Latimer, the FLP endorsed candidate for mayor of Minneapolis.[17]

Nonetheless, Trotsky's abstentionist policies led the leadership of Local 544 to avoid any significant role in the Minnesota Farmer–Labor party from 1930 through 1936. Yet, throughout this period, there was a strong left-wing presence within the FLP. The left-wing faction would have greatly benefited from the backing of Local 544, as it struggled to keep the party independent of the Roosevelt wing of the Democratic party.

Finally in 1937, the Trotskyist activists of 544 found themselves impelled to participate more actively in the FLP. The Communist party had reversed its Third Period policy in 1935 and had entered the FLP. Right after the 1936 elections, the line again shifted, and the CP gave critical support to the New Deal coalition by working within the Democratic party. Thus the Local 544 leadership saw Communist influence steadily increasing within the Minnesota Farmer–Labor party and, furthermore, saw this influence being used in coalition with those who wanted to further dilute the independence of the FLP from the two establishment parties.

To counteract Communist influence, the Trotskyist leadership of Local 544 became embroiled in a pitched fight within the FLP. In the spring of 1937, the Trotskyists gave indirect support to Latimer as he ran for reelection as mayor of Minneapolis. The CIO unions, including those in the Communist orbit, worked for an insurgent candidate in the FLP primary on the basis that Latimer had helped to break a strike through the use of police. From the perspective of the Local 544 leaders, the campaign against Latimer had been instigated by the CP in retaliation for Latimer's endorsement of the American Committee for the Defense of Leon Trotsky. The resulting battle was bitter and divisive, and the final result was the victory of the Republican nominee. In any case, the official Trotskyist policy of abstention from activity within the farmer–labor parties was clearly crumbling.[18]

As long as the Trotskyists remained within the Socialist party, they publicly proclaimed their complete hostility toward the formation of a broadly based reformist party. Yet once the split from the SP finally occurred, the Teamster comrades began to urge Trotsky to drop his previous policy and to support the creation of a labor party.

In April 1938, only a few months after the launching of the Socialist Workers party, Cannon, Shachtman, and Ray Dunne, one of the Minneapolis Teamster leaders, went to Mexico City to discuss independent political action with "The Old Man." Trotsky had come to Mexico in early 1937 in order to live in a country willing to offer exile to Stalin's most hated enemy. Both Dunne and Cannon impressed on Trotsky the need for a more favorable attitude toward independent electoral formations such as the FLP. Shachtman was more dubious, arguing that the highpoint of enthusiasm for independent politics had passed and that this was therefore an inappropriate moment for the SWP to reverse its position.[19]

Trotsky sided with Cannon and the union cadre. He cited two factors, which had unexpectedly changed since his 1930 decision to oppose the formation of a labor party. Trotsky admitted that "I, personally, didn't see that this sharp crisis or series of crises would begin in the next period, and become deeper and deeper." Furthermore, the U.S. working class had responded to the Great Depression with a massive drive toward industrial unionism. Again, "no one in our own ranks foresaw during that period the appearance of the CIO with this rapidity and power." The U.S. working class was therefore confronted with a fundamental dilemma. The economic crisis necessitated a drastic restructuring of society, and, furthermore, the new industrial unions provided the prerequisite base on which to build a powerful working-class movement. Nevertheless, working-class consciousness remained unfocused and the revolutionary Left weak. Trotsky again had to concede that he had "overestimated the possibility of the development of our party at the expense of the Stalinists."

In this situation, a labor party represented a first step out of the dilemma. There was an "objective necessity" for independent political action, since, to defend the gains made by the CIO, "economic action is not enough. We need political action." Thus, "agitation for a working class party is an absolutely concrete task determined by economic and social conditions." Despite the urgent need, Trotsky was very doubtful about the readiness of the CIO hierarchy to break from the two-party system. In his view, the trade union bureaucracy was becoming "more and more disoriented." The CIO leaders were "afraid to break with Roosevelt," and, if the trade union leaders were "not ready for political action," then "we must denounce them."

Trotsky insisted that the SWP should not just agitate for a labor party but that "this party should be an independent party, not for Roosevelt or LaFollette but a machine for the workers themselves." Furthermore, it was essential that the SWP put forward a radical program for such a party, a "transitional program" that "issues from the conditions of capitalist society today, but immediately leads over the limits of capitalism." His suggestions for such a program included demands for worker's control of industry and workers' militias.

In the course of the Mexico City discussions, Trotsky was asked how the SWP could justify its rapid shift on electoral activity. After all, the SWP had recruited part of its current membership from within the Socialist party on the basis of total opposition to socialist advocacy of a labor party. Trotsky glibly answered that this would be "a good school for the comrades. Now they can see dialectical developments better than before."[20]

A plenum of the Socialist Workers party quickly accepted Trotsky's views as its own. It was once again Shachtman, this time with James Burnham, who publicly presented the new position, despite his personal doubts. Shachtman and Burnham began by stressing the possibilities for working-class political activity in that period. Since the "social crisis in the United States is deepening," it followed that "the American workers are certain to move at a faster and clearer pace toward independent political class action."

But "powerful political forces" were blocking such a development. "The leaders of labor, however, strive to confine this movement to the old capitalist parties, that is to prevent this class movement from exceeding the bounds of bourgeois parties, and taking the forms of independent working class political action." The labor leaders were "all deliberately impeding the development of an independent Labor party."

Shachtman and Burnham argued that this obstructionism, while it made the formation of a labor party more difficult, also created a leverage point for revolutionaries within the trade unions. The Trotskyists would now be "positively in favor of the political organization of the U.S. workers as a class, that is of a labor party. This alone makes it possible for us to intervene in the labor movement in such a way as to heighten the class consciousness of the workers, . . . to widen the breach between them and their class-collaborationist, bureaucratic misleadership."

Even should militant rank and file pressure force the union hierarchy to organize an independent party, revolutionaries within it would need to struggle against its control by the union bureaucracy. Union officials would try to "confine it to a safe reformist course," as well as to use it solely as an "instrument to increase their own share of the available plums of power and privilege." For revolutionary socialists, entry into a labor party must be done "in such a way as to develop and advance . . . the fight against the bureaucrats and the liberals." Essential to such a program would be a continuing struggle "against all support of old party candidates."

The new position maintained two links with previous policies. There would be no liquidation of the revolutionary party into a labor party, but rather Trotskyists would insist on joining it as a disciplined faction. Also, the new mass party had to be firmly based on the trade unions in order to ensure that it remained a genuine class party and did not become a "third capitalist party" of the petit-bourgeoisie. Shachtman and Burnham specifically cited the British Labour party as their model and argued that bloc affiliation by the trade unions should be the organizational basis on which the new party was formed.[21]

As had been expected, opposition to the new line came primarily from those who had been recruited out of the Socialist party and especially from among the youth. The chief opposition spokesperson was Hal Draper, an SP recruit and then secretary of the SWP youth section. Draper objected, in part, to the reversal in policy because he doubted that recent events had so fundamentally altered the political scene as to force the Trotskyist tendency to abandon its previous analysis. Specifically, Draper argued that the CIO "is intent upon following its present policy of tailing after the capitalist parties." Hopes for an immediate mass-based break from the two-party system were, therefore, illusory. More fundamentally, Draper argued, U.S. capitalism had "entered the period of an intense social crisis, not one of periodic depressions, which have come and gone, but this is a permanent, chronic crisis of the system itself." Politically, "in periods of sharp social crisis middle grounds crumble away." Indeed, "in this period, a party may be independent of the old capitalist parties . . . in the formal organizational sense, but in the political sense, independence from capitalist politics means revolutionary politics. Here again there is no middle ground." Draper concluded that, given the crisis, "a labor party can play no progressive role." Instead of working for the formation of such a party, Draper proposed as an alternative that "we must begin now laying the ground for the development of soviets."[22]

Despite Draper's objections, most Trotskyists were convinced of the importance of agitating for a broadly based independent party. For Shachtman, the 1938 debate proved to be a turning point as he consistently stressed the necessity of building a labor party for the next 20 years. Trotsky also never hesitated again in his strong support for independent political action, a position he held until his assassination less than three years later. Only Draper remained unconvinced, and, as we shall see later, even he came ultimately to agree on the need for a labor party.

CONCLUSIONS

The Trotskyists carried from their experience within the Communist party a great deal of their basic outlook and political perspective. On one level, this allowed them to remain consistent revolutionaries in opposition to the New Deal, at a time when there was considerable pressure to operate within the liberal coalition. While those who remained within the CP were swept into the Popular Front by mandate of Moscow, the Trotskyists, as a revolutionary socialist organization independent of the Comintern, were able to present a clear and sustained criticism of the realignment perspective of both the CP and the right-wing social democrats.

This assessment has to be counterbalanced by an awareness of very real flaws in the early Trotskyist movement. That Trotsky could reverse the position of the Communist League of America on the necessity for a labor party by offering a few comments from his distant place of exile does not speak well for that organization. Trotsky was hardly in a position to be conversant with the situation in this country, and yet his analysis depended crucially on his assessment of the potential for growth for his fledgling organization.

Eight years later, Trotsky had to admit his mistakes. Yet rather than opening a debate in which the decision to oppose the formation of a labor party could be thoroughly analyzed and similar mistakes avoided in the future, Trotsky and the party leadership just shifted their position and expected that the principles of democratic centralism would lead the membership to accept the new policy. Thus the Trotskyists carried over from the CP a political style that could only have disastrous consequences.

The decision to reject a labor party perspective from 1931 to 1938 also led the Trotskyists to abstain largely from activity within the farmer–labor parties at a time when these parties still had a mass electoral base and a lively internal life. The damage caused by this decision was particularly serious in Minnesota, where the Trotskyists could have taken advantage of their enormous prestige as leaders of the successful Teamster strike of 1934 to promote the Farmer–Labor party and to strengthen the left forces within it. Unfortunately for the cause of independent political action, the Trotskyists continued to denounce the Farmer–Labor party as reformist, even after the Communist party had entered it in force in order to move it further into the orbit of the Democratic party.

Finally, the debate within the Trotskyist tendency was deeply flawed in the polar positions presented as alternative options. In the debate, one could either call for the immediate formation of a mass revolutionary vanguard party or press for the creation of a labor party based on the official union structure. For those who rejected the first position, as Trotsky and most Trotskyists did after 1938, the second perspective contained within it a deeply rooted dilemma. Its proponents were highly critical of the union hierarchy, and yet they still insisted that a new, working class party adopt an organizational structure—bloc voting—that would guarantee to the union leadership total control over party policy.

This underlying tension was to become far more acute in the debates over the next decade within the workers party. Let it suffice to say that the debates within the early Trotskyist tendency lacked a third position, the formation of a radical independent party from below, a party that would have a far less hierarchical structure than has been characteristic of most U.S. trade unions.

NOTES

1. James P. Cannon, *The History of American Trotskyism* (New York: Pioneer, 1944), p. 78.

2. Constance Ashton Myers, *The Prophet's Army* (Westport, Connecticut: Greenwood Press, 1977), pp. 29–32.

3. Theodore Draper, *The Roots of American Communism* (New York: Viking Press, 1957), pp. 137–38, 298, 499.

4. Spector was a founding member of the Canadian Communist party and the editor of its newspaper. Tim Buck, *Reminiscences* (Toronto: NC Press, 1977), pp. 129–32.

5. Myers, *Prophet's Army*, p. 9; Albert Glotzer, "Max Shachtman—A Political-Biographical Essay," *Bulletin of the Tamiment Institute* (April 1983): 3–4.

6. Max Shachtman, *The Militant*, December 1, 1928.

7. *The Militant*, February 15, 1929. This "Platform of the Communist Opposition" was initially signed by Cannon, Shachtman, Arne Swabeck, and Martin Abern, and then passed by the first CLA convention in May 1929.

8. The Comintern memorandum can be found in U.S. Congress, Senate Committee on Foreign Relations, *Recognition of Russia* (Washington, D.C.: GPO, 1924). Lenin also twice advised top leaders of the Communist party to accept the formation of a labor party as a strategic priority. Draper, *Roots of American Communism*, p. 280.

9. In this, too, the CLA was following the path already set by the Communist party. The CP's initial call for a labor party in 1922 already envisioned such a mass party as directly representative of the official trade union structure. Jay Lovestone (Jay Ell), "The Workers Party of America and the United Front," *International Press Correspondence* 2 (June 20, 1922).

10. Leon Trotsky, "Discussions with Max Shachtman," in *Writings of Leon Trotsky, Supplement 1929-33* ed. George Breitman and Sarah Lovell (New York: Pathfinder, 1979), p. 29.

11. *The Militant*, July 25, 1931.

12. Leon Trotsky, "The Labor Party Question" in *Writings of Leon Trotsky*, ed. George Breitman and Sarah Lovell (New York: Pathfinder, 1973), 4: 94–97.

13. Max Shachtman, "The Problem of the Labor Party," *New International* 2 (March 1935): 36–37.

14. Max Shachtman, "Prospects for a Labor Party," *Socialist Appeal* 3 (February 1937): 15–16.

15. Myers, *Prophet's Army*, pp. 123–42.

16. Millard L. Gieske, *Minnesota Farmer-Laborism: The Third Party Alternative* (Minneapolis: University of Minnesota Press, 1979).

17. Farrell Dobbs, *Teamster Politics* (New York: Monad Press, 1975), p. 74.

18. Gieske, *Minnesota Farmer-Laborism*, pp. 211–18, 246–47.

19. Leon Trotsky, *The Transitional Program for Socialist Revolution* (New York: Pathfinder, 1973), pp. 117–36. The citations are from a series of discussions Trotsky held with leading U.S. Trotskyists over the period April–July 1938.

20. Shachtman was correct in this estimate. Independent parties, such as the Farmer–Labor party of Minnesota, did not do well in the 1938 election, and they were further weakened by the approach and advent of World War II. Only toward the end of that war did third-party activity begin to revive.

21. Max Shachtman and James Burnham, "The Question of a Labor Party," *New International* 4 (August 1938): 227–29. Burnham had become a Trotskyist via the merger in 1934 with A.J. Muste's American Workers Party. Burnham played a key role in the 1939–40 controversy, which led to the Workers party, but a month after the formation of the WP he dropped out of Marxist politics. In his later years, Burnham became an ideologue of the right.

22. Hal Draper, "For the Present Party Position," *New International* 4 (August 1938): 229–31.

9
THE WORKERS PARTY AND THE INDEPENDENT SOCIALIST LEAGUE

In 1940, the orthodox Trotskyist movement experienced its deepest and most significant split. A wing of the SWP led by Max Shachtman and including most of the younger activists refused to accept Trotsky's defense of the Soviet invasion of Finland.[1] From that as a starting point, they developed an analysis of the Soviet Union as a new type of exploitative class society, which they termed "bureaucratic collectivism."[2]

Although the new organization formed by the SWP dissidents, the Workers party, never enrolled more than a few hundred members, it did have a considerable influence on the ideological debates within the Left. From the Shachtman tendency came the first formulation of third camp politics, which rejected an identification with either of the superpowers as rival imperialist states and instead urged socialists to ally with mass movements in opposition to both of the competing powers.

The Workers party began its history as an orthodox Leninist formation. It sought to embed itself in the industrial workforce and in particular in the auto industry, where its cadre became activists in the rank and file opposition to the established trade union leadership. Over the 18 years of its existence, the WP, renamed the Independent Socialist League (ISL) in 1949, moved from a position of militant criticism of the union hierarchy and a total rejection of socialist participation within the two-party system to a stance that was far friendlier to the progressive wing of union leaders, such as the UAW's Walter Reuther, and that even called for socialists to support Democratic party candidates in certain specified circumstances. After 1958 and the ISL's merger into the Socialist party, most of its former members went on to adopt explicitly the political perspective of the trade union bureaucracy. Indeed, even now many of the key figures in the Democratic Socialists of America (DSA) and the Social Democrats, USA are former ISL activists.

In tracing the evolution of the WP–ISL, I came to the conclusion that its shifting stance on the crucial issue of socialist participation in the Democratic party could not be understood in isolation from the evolving relationship between the Shachtman tendency and the Reuther wing of the UAW leadership.

WORLD WAR II

The 200 to 300 activists who left the SWP[3] with Shachtman to form the Workers party were convinced that the new party could quickly become the nucleus of a mass-based revolutionary vanguard. Underlying this hope was an analysis of the world scene that was close to apocalyptic. Capitalism was finished, even in its heartland, the United States. Given this, only a socialist revolution could provide a genuine alternative to the world-wide rise of fascism.

In May 1940, one month after the founding convention of the WP, Shachtman wrote that "without socialism, the war of 1939, Hitler victory or no Hitler victory, must inevitably mean the complete destruction of democracy all over Europe, [and] the development of the totalitarian state in America." The impending crisis left no choice, "there is today but one road—speed the revolutionary process."[4]

As for independent politics, the Workers party continued to uphold Trotsky's position of 1938, at least in a formal sense. The party insisted that "an independent party still remains a crying need" and, further, that "the objective conditions and the need of the working class for an independent labor party are over-ripe in this country."[5] Still it is also clear that the perceived need for a labor party clashed with the forecast of an imminent revolutionary crisis. Shachtman was convinced that a "period of social reformist development for the American labor movement, though not excluded, is, at any rate, sure to be of brief duration." The objective basis for reformism no longer existed, since "merely to preserve, not to speak of extending, the social gains of the American workers, the latter will have to engage in the sharpest and most intransigent class struggles." These "to be fruitful and victorious must be guided by a revolutionary party."[6] Thus, although the Workers party officially supported the idea of a broadly based independent class party, it was also convinced that such a party was outdated and that the WP itself could soon become the core of a significant revolutionary party.

Needless to say, as Marxists, those in the WP were well aware that their hopes of rapidly building a revolutionary party depended crucially on their ability to gain support from within the industrial working class. This provided the context for the Workers party program of "colonization," in which many of its members were induced to get factory jobs. In building a presence within the trade union movement, it soon became clear that no union was more important than the UAW.

By 1940, the UAW had passed through its heroic phase, in which it had gained recognition from General Motors and Chrysler through sit-ins and mass mobilizations. When the United States entered World War II, the union's membership was 650,000, and it had become a major force in the auto industry. Furthermore, radicals had played a key role in building the UAW, and there remained a large core of committed and politicized activists.[7]

For revolutionary socialists, the possibilities for gaining positions of influence and for recruiting appeared enormous. The immediate strategy called for the Workers party to aid in the formation of a broadly based rank and file opposition to the union leadership. Once the United States entered World War II, the working class would confront the burden of military expenditures, and "the masses will go to the left." Within the UAW, the WP rejected all alliances with any segment of the union hierarchy. According to B.J. Widick, who was to become a key WP activist in the auto industry, "the attitude of the whole leadership is one of caution and conservatism."[8]

Thus the Workers party began its existence as a tightly disciplined vanguard party, sure of its position and convinced of its potential as a leading element in the revolutionary crisis that was soon to engulf this country, as it already had most of Europe. This perspective was soon to be jettisoned, after the need for a more long-range strategy became obvious.

The WP argument had been that, as a result of the massive militarization of society generated by World War II, the Western democracies "would themselves be converted speedily into totalitarian regimes."[9] Clearly, the WP had greatly underestimated the strength of democratic institutions in the United States. It was Shachtman who first publicly recognized that the party's perspective was mistaken. By April 1941, he was writing that the pressure toward a more totalitarian regime in this country was only a "tendency," one that was balanced by a "counteracting tendency," that is, the defense of democratic rights by the powerful trade union movement.[10]

As Shachtman reversed his position on the likelihood of an authoritarian regime being established in this country, he also came to stress the importance of an independent labor party. Trade union opposition to totalitarian measures could not be restricted to shop-floor militancy but had to be extended to the level of class politics and state power. In Shachtman's words, "unless the American working class speedily develops an independent political party of its own . . . it will be threatened with disintegration and impotence."[11]

By the time of the Workers party's second convention in October 1941, most of its members had decided to support Shachtman's new position. The main convention resolution held that "the workers must have a party of their own, based on the mass organizations of labor."[12] This stress on building a labor party was to be a hallmark of the WP–ISL, a point on which it was to remain firmly committed, even as other important aspects of its political perspective were to undergo fundamental and frequent changes.

Yet once having seriously raised the issue of an independent working class party, the Workers party then had to face a critical question: how would such a party be formed? It was on this key point that much of the changing perspective of Shachtman and the WP turned. During its first years, the Workers party was convinced that only strong pressure from the rank and file could force the union hierarchy to initiate a labor party.

The Workers party insisted that "an independent and militant party of the working class . . . will not be built by the present leaders of the union movement. Too many of them are tied to the boss parties." E.R. McKinney, the WP's labor secretary, argued that "the present leadership is tied body and soul to the capitalist oppressors. The task of political organization is beyond" these union leaders, and thus "they must be replaced."[13]

As the WP dropped its belief in an imminent revolutionary crisis and in the immediate demise of social reformism, it began to analyze more carefully the situation within the trade unions. The party cadre were rapidly discovering the difficulties of building a strong rank and file opposition to the existing leadership of the auto workers union. The UAW had emerged from its initial organizing drives with two caucuses of roughly equal strength. One caucus was led by George Addes, the secretary-treasurer of the union, while the other caucus had as its leading spokesperson Walter Reuther, then vice-president in charge of the GM division. The political differences between the two caucuses were minimal, with considerably greater differences within each caucus than between them. Yet the rivalry was bitter, particularly since the Communist party provided many of the activists in the Addes caucus, while several of the key figures in the Reuther caucus had been active in the Socialist party.

During its first years, the Workers party refused to support either caucus and instead directed its efforts toward building a rank and file grouping that could offer a third, militant alternative to both Reuther and Addes. E.R. McKinney, party spokesperson on labor, observed that "virtually all the most blatant and hidebound reactionaries flocked to the Reuther banner." Indeed, the Reuther caucus "was really a personal 'power caucus' led by union politicians who only wanted to assume control of the international, some of them for personal aggrandizement and prestige." McKinney's view of the factional dispute within the UAW was left unchanged by his attendance at the union's 1942 convention. He found that "no principled differences" existed between the caucuses, but rather

Reuther and Addes were seen as "union bureaucrats [who] are good at internal intrigues and factional fights . . . but they have no stomach for a consistent working class fight."[14]

The Workers party was thus committed to a perspective that emphasized its commitment to militant activity at the shop-floor level and that also minimized the importance of links with the more progressive elements within the union structure. In mid-1943, Shachtman and the Workers party began to shift away from this position and to project a very different perspective, both in terms of theoretical analysis and political practice.

As the 1943 UAW convention neared, the Workers party decided to give the Reuther caucus its critical support in the union's factional disputes. To justify this major reversal in policy, Shachtman relied heavily on anticommunism. Denouncing CP influence within the Addes caucus, Shachtman held that its victory would lead to the destruction of the UAW as an independent working class organization. Since "the natural basis of the Stalinists . . . [was] the Russian rulers who nourish and sustain them," if Addes and the CP were to gain control, the UAW would be emasculated as the Communists relentlessly pursued their policy of increasing production levels for the war against fascism.[15]

Albert Glotzer, the vice-chair of the WP, presented a less sensational rationale for defending the Reuther caucus. He conceded that the Reuther caucus "could hardly be said to have a progressive program. But most progressives now find themselves in or supporting this group." Furthermore, while Glotzer supported the decision to back Reuther against Addes, he also believed that "the most important task before the auto workers is the establishment of a national progressive group" around a radical program, including support for a labor party.[16]

In any case, whether motivated by anticommunism or the desire to establish strengthened ties with the leftwing of the Reuther caucus, the WP had scrapped its policy of neutrality in the factional disputes within the UAW. The decision to give critical support to Reuther was associated with a decided shift in the party's position on independent political action. Until then, the Workers party had been clear that any split from the Democratic party would come despite the desires of the trade union leadership. This was soon no longer the case.

In July 1943, just as the WP was changing its attitude toward Reuther, Shachtman published an article asserting that the increasing pressures on the labor bureaucracy would, in all probability, impel it to break with the two-party system. The self-interest of union officials would spur them to form a labor party in order to defend and extend the power of the trade unions within the capitalist system. Shachtman was sure that there were "powerful forces at work to awaken the political consciousness of the

American working class, but there is no guarantee our primitive minded labor bureaucracy will adapt . . . to the extent of organizing a reformist political party. That is possible, it is even most probable, but it is not absolutely assured,"[17]

Most of those in the Workers party seemed to accept the leadership's new position, and yet, as the party prepared for its third convention, a lively debate developed over the need for independent political action. Hal Draper led the opposition, which criticized Shachtman for advocating the formation of a labor party. Draper still believed that capitalism was rapidly approaching a total economic collapse, and he therefore rejected any call for a labor party as a further barrier to the formation of a mass-based revolutionary party. In his view, out of "the coming post-war collapse of capitalism" there "will come the revolt of the millions," and this will soon bring "the inevitability of a revolutionary wave sweeping the globe."[18]

The Workers party, confronted with the choice between the politics of the apocalypse or Shachtman's version of support for a labor party, chose the latter. A resolution passed by the December 1943 national committee plenum declared that "the struggle for a Labor party is the most important and most urgent political task of the revolutionary vanguard." Furthermore, given the "declining ability of the remnants of 'New Dealism' to give any serious concessions to Labor, or even to the labor officialdom," it was most likely, although not certain, "that the sharpening of class antagonisms in the country will generate enough pressure upon at least a section of the labor bureaucracy to impel it to take the leadership of an independent labor political party."[19]

The position articulated in this resolution represented a significant reversal of the organization's skepticism of the union officialdom's willingness to break with the Democratic party. During the next two years, until the end of the war, the Workers party largely reverted to its initial position of skepticism as the militancy of rank and file workers came into conflict with the cautious stance of the labor leadership.

Left-wing activists in the Reuther caucus had been disgruntled from the beginning with Reuther's decision to join the rest of the UAW leadership in refusing to authorize any strikes for the duration of the war. For the first year or so of massive military production, strike levels remained low and discontent was muted. Then, as the war dragged on and as plant-level grievances went unresolved, shop-floor militancy increased rapidly. Wildcat strikes were frequent in 1943 and reached epidemic levels in 1944, when nearly 400,000 auto workers, nearly half the total number, went on strike at some point during the year.[20]

The response to this militancy from the entire union officialdom, including the leaders of both caucuses, was to crack down on those who led unauthorized strikes. This finally led to a short-lived split in the Reuther caucus. In July 1944, several of the most militant and radical members of the Reuther caucus formed a new group, the Rank and File caucus. The new caucus demanded that the union's executive board reject the no-strike pledge and, instead, give its sanction to local strikes over working conditions. Many key figures in the militant opposition, such as Emil Mazey of Briggs Local 212, had been active in the Socialist party, and they remained committed as socialists to the formation of an independent working class party.[21]

Cadres from the Workers party were active in initially organizing the new caucus and then worked to build it. Shachtman applauded its formation and declared it to have been "a tragic error" that militants in the UAW had ever acted "as mere tails to the kite of either the Reuther or Addes factions."[22]

The Rank and File caucus proved to be an extremely effective vehicle for organizing opposition to the no-strike pledge. At the UAW convention in September 1944, the caucus blocked approval of a resolution reaffirming the pledge, and, when the issue was sent to membership referendum, it led an oppositional campaign that garnered 35 percent of the vote. The caucus not only broke with the no-strike pledge, it also broke with Walter Reuther. Its refusal to endorse him officially contributed to his near defeat for election as UAW vice-president at the 1944 convention.[23]

Through its participation in the Rank and File caucus, the Workers party came into direct conflict with Reuther and the leadership group around him. In conjunction with this break in relations came a subtle, but significant change in the party's perspective on the formation of a labor party. As long as the Workers party gave critical support to Reuther, it held the view that the initial split that would create a new party was likely to stem from the actions of a section of the union hierarchy as it thereby sought to defend itself from the attacks of big business. With the formation of an independent, grass-roots caucus in the UAW, party policy became more ambivalent, as a greater emphasis was placed on the need for rank and file pressure on recalcitrant union officials.

This can be seen most clearly in the response of the Workers party to the formation of the CIO's Political Action Committee (PAC). The CIO executive board had launched PAC in July 1943 in order to counteract the increasingly effective efforts of reactionaries in Congress to roll back the modest gains won by organized labor during the 1930s. The CIO leaders intended PAC to mobilize union members to vote for Roosevelt and liberal Democrats, as well as to divert the growing rank and file demand for independent political action back into the two-party system.[24]

At first, the Workers party generally ignored PAC, although in March 1944 Herman Benson criticized the CIO leadership because "the policy of PAC is to function as a labor adjunct of the Democratic Party."[25] Yet, as the 1944 election drew closer, it became clear that PAC was a serious force in the election and that the CIO was determined to sustain it as a permanent factor in U.S. politics. The response of Shachtman and the other leaders of the Workers party to these developments was indicative of the underlying ambiguity in their attitudes toward the official union structure, as intensified by WP participation in the Rank and File caucus.

In October 1944, Shachtman wrote that "the mere emergence of the PAC, even though as a constituent part of the Democratic Party" had increased the possibilities for an independent party. This was because "PAC is a stage in the development of Labor as an independently organized political party."[26] Although Shachtman still believed that external pressures would tend to move union officials toward a break with the two-party system, he had become more cautious in this assessment. It was also essential for union militants to prod the leadership continually, to "fight for transforming the PAC from an instrument of the bosses to a political instrument of the working class, i.e. to transform the PAC into a Labor Party."[27] Others in the Workers party were even clearer on the need to overcome the opposition of the CIO leadership if PAC were to break with the Democratic party. Emmanuel Geltman felt certain that "PAC must be forced by the pressure of labor's ranks to free itself of its capitalist party ties."[28]

THE POSTWAR PERIOD

Throughout the war, the Workers party had remained firmly committed to a revolutionary politics, despite the flirtation with Reuther in 1943. The postwar economic boom came as a tremendous shock to the Shachtman tendency, as it did to most U.S. socialists. It soon became clear that the United States was entering a period of political stability and that a significant upsurge in the revolutionary movement was not on the horizon. The growing mood of cynicism was heightened by the cooptation of the UAW's leftwing back into the Reuther caucus and the consolidation of power by the Reuther machine within the UAW structure.

The process began with the GM strike of 1945–46 and the election of Reuther as UAW president in March 1946. Reuther was director of the union's GM division and was thus in a key position to determine strategy during the crucial period immediately after the end of the war. He knew that he could only regain his popularity with the ranks if he adopted a militant posture toward the dominant corporation in the auto industry.

The result was a 113 day strike, which Reuther presented as a bitter struggle for the "GM Program." The union's initial demands were for a 30 percent increase in wages with no increase in car prices. When GM responded that this was impossible, Reuther challenged the giant firm to "open the books" so that everyone could see its excessively high profits and could be assured of its ability to pay higher wages from them. With Reuther insisting that he would refuse to budge from these demands, the strike dragged on through the winter of 1945–46.[29]

During the strike, Shachtman signalled a change in WP policy. Soon after the GM strike had been called, he strongly praised the GM program since it marked "a new level of social consciousness for American labor."[30] Needless to say, Reuther finally settled with GM without having gained access to the books and for the wage pattern already set in steel. He never again raised "open the books" as a demand, but by then he had succeeded in his drive to become UAW president.

The GM strike and the 1946 UAW convention that soon followed it confronted the Workers party with a difficult choice. During the last years of the war, the WP had been highly critical of Reuther, and, indeed, just before the 1946 convention, E.R. McKinney, its labor secretary, had written that whether R.J. Thomas, the incumbent president backed by the Addes–CP caucus, "is re-elected or whether he is replaced by Reuther is not really of any basic importance."[31] The WP cadre in the auto industry, however, had developed real links with many of the leading activists of the Rank and File caucus. This group of local leaders had long-standing ties with Reuther, despite the open break over the no-strike pledge at the 1944 convention. The militant stance taken by Reuther during the GM strike had restored his reputation in the eyes of shop-floor militants and thus had made it easy for most of those who had been active in the Rank and File caucus to rejoin the Reuther caucus quietly as its leftwing.[32]

As a result, even before the 1946 UAW convention convened, the Rank and File caucus had dwindled away, leaving the Workers party adrift. At first, although the WP recognized that "support is flowing back into the channels of the two big" caucuses, it continued to refuse to support either caucus. Just before the start of the convention, the Workers party reversed its position and began to support Reuther, although with reservations. To justify this switch, the Workers party argued that "Reuther was elected president because he was associated with a program of militant and advanced action in the GM strike." Advancing the GM program had ensured that Reuther "became the center of attraction for militants and progressives," even though the militants "knew that Reuther would not carry this program through."[33]

While almost all of the leadership of the Workers party endorsed the decision to support Reuther in his successful campaign to become UAW president, most of them also continued to be skeptical of his intentions and critical of the union hierarchy in general. Albert Glotzer, vice-chair of the WP, wrote in the latter part of 1946 that the formation "of a labor party will require the breakdown of the conservative influence of the officialdom."[34] A similar view was expressed by Geltman, who was sure that neither Phillip Murray, the head of the CIO, or Walter Reuther would "issue the call" to independent political action, so that "we must promote the formation of a Labor Party through our own activity."[35]

Shachtman was less critical of Reuther and of union officials in general. In terms of the UAW, he pledged the Workers party as "the enthusiastic champions of the GM program." The party "must at every stage try to mobilize support for Reuther" on the basis of the GM program, although, of course, Shachtman recognized that Reuther would not, "and being what he is, could not conduct a consistent struggle for this program."[36]

Overall, Shachtman's attitude toward the labor bureaucracy moved back toward his 1943 position, as he again gave active support to the Reuther caucus within the UAW. For instance, he insisted that an independent party should be "based upon and organized by the trade unions, as the most democratic . . . of the social organizations in the country."[37] Obviously, if the existing trade unions were models of democracy, socialist support for rank and file insurgencies became less urgent.

The attitude of the WP toward the UAW leadership and toward the labor bureaucracy in general was ambivalent in the period from early 1946 through mid-1947. The final consolidation of Reuther's dominance in the union then led to a further shift in WP policy. Although Reuther had been elected president in 1946, a majority of the executive board continued to back the Addes–CP caucus. The union was split down the middle and in a state of virtual warfare, as both sides prepared for the decisive 1947 convention. The internal political life of the UAW had become bitterly polarized, and the issue of Communist intervention in the union became a focal point for the divisiveness. With the United States entering the postwar wave of anticommunist hysteria, Reuther, too, employed red-baiting as a major weapon in his drive to consolidate his power within the UAW.[38]

Unfortunately, the Workers party became trapped in the internecine clash of the two caucuses. Initially, the WP had entered the Reuther caucus as its extreme leftwing, with its ties to the group around Emil Mazey rather than to Reuther directly. In 1947, as the two caucuses were locked in their final battle, the Workers party linked itself directly to the Reuther camp. The Workers party depended heavily on attacks on Communist influence in the opposition caucus as justification for its all-out support for Reuther at the 1947 convention. For Shachtman, "Stalinism today is the greatest, best organized, most persistent and poisonous danger to the labor movement."[39]

E.R. McKinney, in an article aimed at the UAW convention delegates, wrote that "the Stalinist party crouches in the background, with poised dagger, to stab your international in the back and deliver it to the control of the

GPU."[40] Even after the Addes–CP caucus was routed by a margin of two to one, McKinney continued to call for a further campaign against Communist influence in the UAW. In his view, "anyone who suggests or winks at compromise is only aiding and abetting the Stalinists."[41]

While hostility to the Communist party helped draw the Workers party closer to Reuther, more fundamental were its increasingly close ties to the progressive wing of the Reuther caucus. Herman Benson, who along with McKinney was the WP's leading authority on labor, argued that "the Reuther tendency by and large, is based upon and receives its stamp from the forward moving radical and progressive elements" in the UAW. Shachtman also defended his support for Reuther on this basis. Because of Reuther's identification with the GM program, "the great bulk of the most advanced and progressive militants are to be found . . . in the Reuther camp." B.J. Widick was even more specific, as he defended participation in the Reuther caucus on the basis that "it contains pro-Labor Party groupings."[42]

The Workers party was particularly encouraged by the outcome of the 1947 convention when Emil Mazey was resoundingly elected secretary-treasurer. Mazey had been a sparkplug of the Unemployed Councils during the 1930s and then became the president of Briggs Local 212, famous for its militant strikes and radical politics. Mazey was a staunch proponent of independent political action, and in 1947 he was still a nominal member of the Socialist party.[43]

Workers party cadre were hopeful that Mazey "would be the aggressive spokesman for a more militant and radical wing of the Reuther group."[44] His voice in the inner circle would provide the essential spark that would move the UAW to break from the Democratic party. Mazey would be able to use the status of his position, the second most powerful in the union, to promote his belief in the need for a labor party. Given this left pressure from within and the general disillusionment with Truman among the rank and file, Reuther and the UAW would be propelled into acting as the focal point in the formation of a new party.

This scenario was put to the test by the 1948 presidential election, and it was found wanting. The Communist party had been urging liberals to split from the dominant, Cold War wing of the Democratic party since the disintegration of the wartime alliance between the Soviet Union and the United States. The CP still had considerable influence within the CIO and in the wider grouping of progressive organizations as well. From this base came the Progressive party, which had as its presidential candidate Henry Wallace, FDR's vice-president from 1940 to 1944.[45]

From start to finish, the Workers party publicly attacked the Progressive party and the Wallace campaign. It portrayed Wallace as a "pro-Stalinist appeaser" and insisted that the Wallace effort "is a Stalinist inspired campaign and exists in actual life only as a Stalinist creature."[46]

Dismay at Communist influence was not the only factor underlying the attacks of the WP on the Progressive party. Again, events in the UAW influenced the organization's policy. The Workers party was convinced that Reuther was about to break from the Democratic party in order to launch a major third party effort, one that would render the Progressive party an irrelevant shell. In March 1948, the UAW executive board reinforced these hopes by approving a resolution stating that the union "adopts as its official political objective the formation after the 1948 election of a genuine progressive political party." Although the WP focused on this part of the resolution, it tended to ignore the union's activities during the next months of the 1948 campaign. United Auto Workers funds were funneled to liberal Democrats running for Congress, and in September the union reluctantly endorsed Truman. Even at the March 1948 executive board meeting, Reuther made it clear that the resolution advocating a new third party was a political guideline and not a call for immediate action. One clause of the resolution initiated a union educational program to promote independent political action, "looking forward to the time when its practical implementation is possible." Reuther interpreted this to mean that a third party was a good idea, "you got to have one," but only at some unspecified time in the future. That is, "whenever it is practical, but it can't be *before.* That's the point."[47]

Despite these clear signs of the UAW hierarchy's reluctance to definitively break with the Democratic party, the Workers party was convinced that the union was committed to the formation of an independent party once the elections were over. In August 1948, Emmanuel Geltman assured the comrades that "there is every reason to believe that Reuther will live up to his commitment."[48]

Shachtman reflected this optimism in a draft resolution on the U.S. political scene prepared in September 1948 for the organization's 1949 convention. He viewed the UAW resolution and the popular support for the Wallace campaign as proofs that "the formation of a national labor party is now on the horizon." Union officials had come to understand the need to create an independent party as a defense against the increasingly sharp attacks of big business. "There is less and less reason every day for thinking that the reformist labor leadership of the United States will fail to take the political road of its similars in virtually all the other capitalist countries of the world."

Shachtman continued to hold that the Workers party should remain outside of the Progressive party, but he now admitted that Wallace had gained "broad mass support" and that his campaign "is the most important development to occur . . . in years." Of course, Shachtman remained sharply critical of the dominant role of the CP in the Progressive party, but he also urged the WP to "support every progressive opposition to the

Stalinist program" from within the Progressives. The organizational alliance between independent leftists and Communist party cadre was bound to disintegrate in the near future, which made it even more essential for the WP to be in contact with those independents.

The Wallace campaign also led Shachtman to reassess his views on the likely organizational structure of a new party. He no longer held that such a party would be "formally composed of and based upon the mass trade unions," but rather such a party would be a membership organization, such as the Progressive party. Still, a successful third party required the active support of at least a significant section of the official trade union structure. Shachtman concluded "that there is a wide base of support for an independent third party," but that such a party could only arise from "a coalescence" of the Reuther tendency of union officials and "the non-Stalinist elements of the Wallace party."[49]

Shachtman's draft resolution was revised in the political committee, apparently to meet the objections of Hal Draper. Draper had dropped his opposition to advocating the formation of a labor party when the postwar economic collapse he had expected failed to materialize. He now accepted much of the strategic perspective of the majority, although he was also concerned about the continuing rightward drift in Shachtman's politics.

The final version of the resolution, as passed by the Workers party at its 1949 convention, retained the essence of Shachtman's analysis, but it also explicitly argued that socialists would need to act "as the left-wing of labor's third party movement," and, in this role, the revolutionary Left "will seek to push the movement even further, in program, democratic control by the trade union rank and file, independence, not only from the old capitalist parties, but from capitalist politics, and militancy in action."[50]

In the end, the WP had missed its best chance to work within a mass-based third party by its refusal to support the Wallace campaign. Instead, it opted to pursue a de facto alliance with the UAW leadership, all in the vain hope that the Reuther tendency was about to break from the Democratic party.

These hopes for a quick breakthrough in independent political action were quickly discovered to be illusions. Only two months after the election, Benson had to concede that Reuther "thinks only of remaining as a supporter of the Truman Democrats, trusting in their promises."[51] Reuther's open adherence to the Democratic party only convinced Shachtman of the need to modify his position further, although this only became evident a year or so later.

At the 1949 convention, the name of the organization was changed to the Independent Socialist League (ISL). The change reflected a recognition that the organization was primarily a "propaganda group" and not an effective disciplined vanguard party.[52] By then the WP held a political perspective that differed significantly from that which it had originally articulated on its formation. Although this ongoing political evolution had been a slow one, it had generated a certain dissatisfaction with WP policy within the ranks.

Criticisms of the majority position came from those with very different viewpoints. Several members objected to the continued support for Walter Reuther, even after the Reuther caucus had smashed the influence of the Communist party within the UAW. On the other hand, a small minority felt that Shachtman was not moving rapidly enough to a full acceptance of the policies and perspective of Reuther and the progressive wing of the union hierarchy, and that the ISL should support the progressive forces within the Democratic party.

Opposition to the organization's continued ties to the Reuther caucus only came into the open in 1948, after Reuther had solidified his total control over the union apparatus. One of the comrades observed that Reuther had "now reduced to a militant phrase" his support for the GM program.[53] Gordon Haskell, one of the ISL's leading members, rejected Shachtman's argument that socialists should always ally with social democrats in trade union factional disputes in which the other caucus has ties to the CP. In calling for a "third camp" position within trade unions, he pointed out that Communist union officials do "not necessarily and in all instances saddle on the workers in the unions . . . a regime any more bureaucratic and totalitarian than do bourgeois leaders."[54]

Even a part of the WP–ISL leadership had doubts about the increasingly close ties to the UAW leadership. E.R. McKinney had been an enthusiastic backer of the Reuther caucus from 1946 through 1948, but by 1949 he had to concede that "there is no one in the top leadership of the unions today who can be depended on to take an independent stand for independent political action." Even Emil Mazey, the great hope of the Workers party, had "folded-up" after his election as UAW secretary-treasurer.[55]

Despite the skepticism of some comrades toward the UAW leadership, the official position of the WP–ISL continued to be one of friendly support mixed with mild criticism. Herman Benson, as an observer at the 1949 UAW convention, reported that "the vast majority of militants in the UAW are now behind Reuther" in order "to achieve a militant and democratic program." Benson concluded that "the UAW is unquestionably one of the most democratic unions in the United States."[56]

For those at the other pole who criticized the organization for its timidity in moving toward Reuther and his policies, the key question was the Democratic party and the attitude of socialists toward it. For instance, Susan Green, who had been well within the mainstream of the Workers party in its early years, was a proponent of realignment politics by early 1950.

Entry into the Democratic party was, she argued, "a purely operational" decision, which should occur whenever this "would further the particular objectives the ISL sets." Having reduced independent political action to a strictly tactical question, Green went on to suggest that the southern conservative Democrats could be forced out of that party, and thus "the leftist tendencies within the Democratic Party would be strengthened." The resulting political realignment would leave the situation in the United States "not too far removed from the conservative and labor divisions in politics in England."[57] Green's position and that currently advanced by socialists such as Michael Harrington are strikingly similar.

In 1950, only a few of those in the ISL were in basic agreement with Green's viewpoint. Over the next two years, several members who shared this perspective either quit the ISL or became inactive. The most prominent person in this loose group was Irving Howe, the influential literary critic and author. Howe has become one of the officially recognized spokespeople for the Left, as well as an active member of the Democratic Socialists of America.[58]

Despite these undercurrents of discontent, the great majority of the ISL supported Shachtman, and the leadership's resolution was passed with little opposition at the 1949 convention. Internal debates were to become considerably more intense after the Willoughby Abner case.

The new controversy began at the end of 1949, when Shachtman proposed a further shift in ISL electoral policy. Since the 1944 elections, the Workers party had been urging the CIO to transform its Political Action Committee into a labor party. Five years later, Shachtman took this argument considerably further. Socialists should continue to insist on the importance of labor breaking its ties with the established parties, but "where the policy of supporting the candidates of a capitalist party is adopted by the unions, it would be correct for the left-wing to propose that the unions at least put forward their own candidates for the nominations . . . and organize a fight for these candidates in the primary elections." In these circumstances, the left wing would be correct in "pledging its support of the union nominees, if they win in the primaries." Shachtman argued that union-backed candidates within the Democratic party would "deepen and sharpen the conflict of interests between the bureaucracy of the official capitalist parties and the labor leadership . . . contributing to a separation between them."[59]

With all the qualifications and restrictions, Shachtman was proposing that the ISL be prepared, in certain circumstances, to enter the Democratic party in alliance with the labor leadership, although with the sole purpose of advancing the time when labor would finally split from the Democrats. Of course, this represented a significant reversal of previous WP–ISL policy, and it initiated an intense debate within the organization. Shachtman advanced his proposal at a plenum of the national council in late 1949, where it was countered by a resolution from Herman Benson.

Benson opposed any support for Democratic party candidates, holding that Shachtman's position would result in the ISL "abandoning the slogan for a Labor Party completely, in practice, or relegating it to an unimportant place."[60] In essence, Benson argued that the ties of the trade union to the Democratic party were so tight that the union leadership would interpret a decision by ISL cadre to work for union activists who ran within the Democratic primary as a commitment by the ISL to accept fully the constraints of the two-party system.

Shachtman's proposal was not accepted by the national council, but the issues he had raised were to reappear quickly. Soon after the plenum, the Chicago branch requested permission to endorse Willoughby Abner as a Democratic nominee for the Illinois state senate. Abner was a black activist, a UAW staff representative, and the leading spirit in organizing a functioning PAC group in the south-side Chicago ghetto.

The arguments within the national council concerning the Abner endorsement were very similar to those at the previous plenum. Shachtman argued that the ISL should back Abner, since his campaign "represents, not in form but in essence, not in full but in part, labor's self-reliance and independence in the political field." Benson, acting again as chief spokesperson for the opposition, pointed out that Abner had run his campaign as a loyal Democrat and not as a candidate of labor. Indeed, "the role of the Democratic Party put him [Abner] forward not as a labor opponent of the Truman administration, but as the best local representative of continued alliance with it." Abner's own campaign literature, according to Benson, assured the voters that he would "be a positive, urgent force to . . . help Governor [Adlai] Stevenson," then governor of Illinois.[61]

This time, those holding the middle position in the debate sided with Shachtman, and Abner was endorsed by the ISL. A spokesperson for the Middle defended the endorsement as appropriate, given the specific and unusual circumstances. Abner had been instrumental in forming a PAC local in south-side Chicago, which functioned as an ongoing organization and not just as a vehicle to gain the support of Black voters for liberal Democrats at election time. Given that Abner was the representative of "a genuine, year-round political action movement," it was necessary for the ISL to "deviate from our labor party position."[62]

Despite the rationalizations, the Abner case marked another substantial shift in WP-ISL policy. The pressure to reach an understanding with progressive elements within the official union structure had led the organization to soften its total commitment to independent political action. Underlying the shift in position was a deep-seated skepticism about the likelihood of a powerful rank and file movement within the unions. B.J.

Widick, in *Labor Action's* 1950 *May Day* issue, admitted that "candor compels us to state that in the coming period no effective new leadership to challenge the old appears likely to arise."[63] Given this, the only meaningful role for socialists was to act as a left pressure group on the Reuther tendency of union officials.

We have examined the evolution of WP-ISL policy from 1940 through 1950 in considerable detail, but our overview of the final eight years of the ISL will be far briefer. I would argue that by 1950 most of its members had come to accept a political perspective that fundamentally oriented toward the progressive wing of the trade union leadership. Although the Korean War led the ISL to halt momentarily its rightward drift, with the end of the war, the organization reverted to its previous policies. In a real sense, the ISL marked time after 1950, as Shachtman and his supporters sought a more promising organizational vehicle from which to promote their perspective. The disintegration of the Communist party in 1956 gave Shachtman his opportunity, and he took it.

THE KOREAN WAR AND ITS AFTERMATH

As it happened, the change in electoral policy implied by the endorsement of Abner was to be temporarily reversed by the ISL during the Korean War. Within two weeks of the start of hostilities, the ISL issued a statement denouncing "the ravishing of Korea by the imperialist rivals. We urge the labor movement . . . to proclaim its complete independence from the imperialist policy of the American government."[64]

The organization's forthright stand led to a break in relations with the UAW leadership. Reuther's support for U.S. intervention in Korea led him to oppose any action that could obstruct the war effort. By an unfortunate coincidence, the UAW had signed a five-year contract with GM just one month before the outbreak of hostilities. With war came rapid inflation and tremendous discontent within the ranks. For two years, Reuther kept a tight check on shop-floor militancy as real wages fell. Finally in 1952, with the war at a deadlock, Reuther demanded a reopening of the contract and backed up this demand by sanctioning local strikes. General Motors reluctantly agreed to a contract revision in May 1953.[65]

The ISL's attitude toward the UAW hierarchy became more critical during the war. Herman Benson reported on the 1951 convention, where "the issue of democracy is more sharply and delicately posed than ever before." B.J. Widick, one of the ISL cadre in the auto plants, argued that "the gap between the international union machine and the ranks is getting bigger." This gap reflected the basic problem of the UAW leaders, "their dilemma of sacrificing for the national defense."[66] Again, as in 1944–45, conflict with the Reuther tendency tended to act as a brake to the ISL's drift toward a partial acceptance of organized labor's role in the Democratic party. The 1951 ISL convention denounced the union officialdom for "class collaboration" in its support for the Korean War. Nonetheless, the ISL still believed that "the antagonisms between the labor bureaucracy on the one hand and the bourgeois state and parties on the other remain as a striking symptom of those class conflicts which will lead to a rupture between labor and the capitalist class." Thus the ISL remained convinced that the attacks of big business on the trade unions would force the labor leadership to split from the Democratic party. Still the 1951 convention, under the impetus of the Korean War, reversed the policy set by the national committee in the Abner case. "The convention rejects the proposal that the ISL or its friends advocate or support labor's contesting in the primaries of the bourgeois parties, and rejects support to candidates running on the ticket of the bourgeois parties."[67]

As the Korean War wound down and the country returned to peacetime conditions, the controversies that had provoked the break with the UAW hierarchy began to fade in importance. Independent Socialist League commentaries on the UAW became distinctly less critical of the Reuther leadership. Benson reported that, at the union's 1953 convention, "The Reutherite leadership displayed its distinctive character as the most radical wing in the labor movement." Indeed, Benson concluded, "the UAW remains the most progressive and democratic union in the United States."[68]

Accompanying this renewal of a positive approach to the Reuther tendency was a further erosion in the ISL's opposition to working within the Democratic party. The 1954 convention overturned the decision of the previous convention and finally accepted Shachtman's position. The main resolution proposed to the convention urged ISL activists to press their unions "to fight for their own candidates, from the ranks of labor and responsible to it, even in the Democratic Party." Shachtman, with Albert Glotzer and Gordon Haskell, then successfully amended the resolution so that "the categorical prohibition against ISL support for such candidates . . . which was adopted at the last convention of the League is no longer operative."[69] Thus the Abner exception had become general policy.

Once the Korean War had ended, the ISL's faith in Walter Reuther was unshakeable. Indeed, even in 1954, when Reuther denounced any third-party effort and insisted on the need to "work within the two-party system of America and thus bring about within the two party system a fundamental realignment of basic political forces,"[70] ISL policy remained unchanged.

At first flush, Gordon Haskell harshly criticized Reuther's statement as indicative of "Reuther's conversion to a completely standardized liberal-bourgeois view of American society." Indeed, "the air may be cleared of at least one illusion: that some kind of leadership can be expected from them in the direction of the formation of a labor party." B.J. Widick, a long-time ISL activist in the auto industry, was also dismayed by Reuther's comments. Many on the Left had hoped that the UAW leaders were "socialists at heart." Now it was necessary "to recognize that the Reuther cadre, consciously, deliberately, and with many discussions, have broken with their ideas" and were totally committed to working within the Democratic party.[71]

Reuther's statement was an excellent opportunity for a fundamental reevaluation of ISL policy toward the UAW. The organization had taken at face value Reuther's vague statements on the need for a labor party. Independent Socialist League cadre had backed him in the factional conflict with the Addes–CP caucus and had, in general, praised his policies in administering the union. All this because the ISL was convinced that, when push came to shove, Reuther would break with his liberal allies and support a third party.

Nonetheless, despite Reuther's explicit statement and soon after the disillusioned comments quoted above, the ISL reverted to its previous position and continued its praise of Reuther's policies. Widick soon resumed writing of the UAW as "the vanguard sector of the labor movement." Herman Benson not only argued that "the UAW is far ahead of most other unions," but he stubbornly insisted that "now is the time for the UAW to raise its old banner: for a new progressive party."[72]

The ISL was marked by hesitancy and timidity after 1950. Shachtman had succeeded in winning most of the members over to his position, but the position itself was a tentative and ambiguous one. Furthermore, as time went on, the ISL cadres became increasingly dissatisfied with the organization, as it stagnated in numbers and as the commitment of the initial core group dwindled. Still, as long as there seemed to be no meaningful alternative, the ISL stumbled on, waiting and looking for a way out.

Events in the Soviet Union had consistently divided the Left in this country, starting with the disastrous split of the Socialist party in 1919. But in 1956 the pattern appeared to be turning around. The impact of Khrushchev's revelations of Stalin's regime of terror and the Soviet invasion of Hungary led to mass resignations from the Communist party, as most of its members and much of its leadership left in disgust. For Shachtman, this was the golden opportunity for a new beginning.

The ISL had been in contact with left-wing members of the SP for several years, hoping in this way to encourage the SP to adopt a more radical stance. Several delegates to the June 1956 Socialist party convention, including David McReynolds, proposed a merger between the ISL and the SP. The proposal was defeated by a vote of three to one, primarily because Norman Thomas and others in his wing of the party were certain that the SP would be swamped by former ISL cadre.[73]

As it happened, these developments coincided with Khrushchev's secret speech on the Stalin era and the Poznan revolt of Polish workers. For the first time in years, Shachtman and the ISL saw a genuine possibility of building a broadly based socialist organization, one that would contain a variety of tendencies, including Third Camp revolutionary socialism. In their view, the SP provided the most likely organizational framework for such a broad regroupment.

In November 1956, the ISL Political Committee enthusiastically responded to the initiative of the SP left wing. The ISL explained that its eagerness to link up with the SP did not represent "a temporary or conjunctural expedient" and that the ISL was firmly committed to furthering "a lasting regroupment of socialist forces." One potential hurdle to the proposed regroupment was the state of the SP. By 1956, the Socialist party had less than 1,000 members, and it was far from being a dynamic organization. It was clear to everyone concerned that the former members of the ISL had the ability to dominate a merged organization. In order to allay the fears of those in the SP, ISL leaders repeatedly promised that their group would not force its views on a regrouped organization and, indeed, that they foresaw the new organization as a loose federation. Its unity would be based on a common understanding of one fundamental principle, that socialism necessarily implied a radical extension of democratic rights and thus that dictatorial societies were inherently not socialist societies.[74]

Merger with the Socialist party was bound to be an appealing perspective to ISL activists. Third camp politics would be able to break out of the narrow base set by a small propaganda group, and, instead, these politics would become a focal point for a legitimate tendency within a broader socialist formation. Nevertheless, there were those who were strongly opposed to this position, among them Hal Draper who attacked Shachtman's proposals on unity as "a systematic adaptation to social democracy."[75] Draper criticized Shachtman for being so anxious to merge with the SP that he sought to mute the key differences in viewpoint between the ISL and the dominant, Norman Thomas wing of the Socialist party. Furthermore, Draper charged, once in the regrouped organization, Shachtman would work to block debates on the critical issues, so as to avoid serious conflicts with the more moderate elements within the broad grouping.

Draper's point was confirmed by Shachtman's shifting position on the Democratic party, as put forward in a resolution submitted by the ISL leadership to its 1957 convention. Until then, the Independent Socialist League had focused its efforts on pushing labor to run its own candidates, even if as Democrats. Of course, in the great majority of cases, PAC and then the AFL-CIO's COPE had supported liberal Democratic politicians and not union activists. The ISL had resolutely opposed these endorsements, but now its opposition began to wane.

The leadership resolution proposed that the ISL should not "as a rule, favor that socialists run candidates in opposition to those endorsed by the labor movement, even when it endorses bourgeois candidates." Such a policy would avoid "giving anyone a chance of accusing them falsely of sabotaging the political effort of the labor movement."[76]

To Draper, the proposed policy shift was another sign of the ISL leadership's willingness to tailor its policies to those of the right wing of the SP. He argued instead that "far from considering that such a socialist campaign is a bad thing because it counterposes socialists to the official labor bureaucracy, or the bourgeois candidates supported by the official labor movement, we would urge it as a good thing."[77]

The convention tabled both of the conflicting resolutions, since the issue was obviously contentious and, in any case, the organization was about to dissolve. Although the ISL voted nearly unanimously at its 1957 convention to enter the SP, the merger issue bitterly divided the Socialist party. After a prolonged fight of over a year, the party narrowly approved a plan to absorb those in the ISL as individual members.[78]

Even as it voted to dissolve, the ISL reaffirmed in principle its commitment to independent political action. The 1957 convention resolution on joining the SP held that the regrouped organization "must permit the cooperate coexistence" of those who opposed working for Democratic party nominees and those "who would support bourgeois candidates under certain conditions." Yet the ISL still projected itself as a focal point for a left-wing tendency within the regrouped Socialist party. The ISL resolution proposed that the SP adopt as its stand "that one of the primary tasks of a socialist organization is to clearly and unambiguously, as an organization, oppose support to the capitalist parties and candidates and to dispel illusions about the possibilities of working within, defending or reforming one or the other as the lesser evil."[79]

From the summer of 1957 to the fall of 1958, as the ISL waited expectantly to join the SP, ISL leaders went even further in their efforts to avoid any conflict with the right wing of the Socialists. In March 1958, Shachtman suggested that the SP "take the position that any local or state socialist body which wants to do so should be permitted to help labor and liberals in these [Democratic Party] primaries. In time, it is my belief, labor and liberals will see that their only road is independent political action."[80]

Soon afterward, Herman Benson indicated that the ISL would back candidates within the Democratic party who had close ties to the more progressive wing of the union bureaucracy. Benson reiterated the ISL's belief that socialists who fully entered the Democratic party "would tend to become ordinary liberals." Although he continued to uphold the principle of independent political action, Benson still argued that "at every stage they [socialists] should seek to participate in politics together with the labor movement or sections of it, to push it forward against the old-line party machines, and stimulate such party struggles as lead, in the end, away from the coalition . . . that constitutes the Democratic Party and toward a new party."[81]

Thus as the ISL dissolved into the SP, those in the ISL majority retained only a formal adherence to a politics independent of the two-party system. Their deepening ties to the Reuther wing of the union leadership had cleared the way for their entry into the Democratic party, despite their continuing doubts as to whether the Democrats could indeed be transformed into a party of the working class. This final barrier to a full acceptance of realignment politics quickly disintegrated once the ISL was absorbed into the Socialist party.

At the other pole, the oppositional group around Draper soon left the SP and formed the Independent Socialist Clubs, out of which came the International Socialists. Ironically, the ISL ended as the Workers party had begun. Shachtman had been in a distinct minority in the Socialist Workers party at the time of the 1940 split, and yet most of the SWP's youth went with Shachtman into the Workers party. Draper had been virtually alone within the ISL leadership in his opposition to the organization's rightward drift, and yet he, too, gained the support of a significant number of the ISL's young activists, who joined with him in a continuing commitment to a revolutionary socialist politics.

CONCLUSIONS

Shachtman's decision to push for the ISL's absorption into the Socialist party came as a bitter shock to Draper and the left-wing opposition. They argued that this represented an abandonment of the revolutionary politics that the Workers party, and then the Independent Socialist League, had consistently articulated since its formation in 1940.

My analysis of the WP–ISL has shown that Draper's view is untenable. Shachtman's position of 1956 did not represent a sharp break with his past, but rather it constituted a further incremental step in an ongoing political evolution. Draper was correct in assessing Shachtman's perspective as "an adaptation to social democracy," but, in fact, the organization had been adapting its politics to those on its right for many years.

Indeed, the ISL had confronted a fundamental dilemma. The majority tendency was eager to work with Walter Reuther and the more progressive wing of the union hierarchy, even if this meant entering the Democratic party. Yet everyone in the ISL agreed on the crucial need for an independent party of labor. Initially, this conflict was resolved by holding that the increasingly bitter attacks from the capitalist class would soon force the union leadership into a more militant stance and would compel them into understanding the futility of continued ties to the Democrats. When this scenario proved to be incorrect, the ISL was left drifting, as it haltingly grouped toward an accommodation with the Reuther forces.

Still, the continued existence of the ISL as an independent organization acted as a sharp brake to the rightward drift in its politics. After all, the organization had consistently stressed the crucial importance of independent political action, and, even in its last years during the 1956 election, the ISL continued to attack the entire union leadership for its strong ties to the Democratic party.

The dilemma that confronted the majority tendency could not be resolved within the organizational constraints set by the ISL. Once having entered the Socialist party, Shachtman and his supporters quickly and totally adopted the perspective of working within the Democratic party. Soon those who had been in the ISL were the SP's most fervent backers of the Kennedy–Johnson administration. As ideologues trained in the Trotskyist tradition, the task of fully refining and articulating the politics of realignment fell on the shoulders of these former revolutionary socialists.

SOURCES

I have depended primarily on the organization's own literature for the forgoing analysis. The Workers party, and later the ISL, issued a theoretical magazine, the *New International*, and an agitational paper, *Labor Action*. It also printed internal documents, including an internal discussion bulletin, circulars, and reports. These latter have been collated by Hal Draper as *Independent Socialist Mimeographia* (Berkeley, California: Independent Socialist Press, 1971) or, in reference, *Mimeographia*. Interviews with Draper and Joel Geier helped me to understand better the WP–ISL, but, wherever possible, I have relied on the printed record.

NOTES

1. Constance Ashton Myers, *The Prophet's Army* (Westport, Connecticut: Greenwood, 1977), pp. 152–65.

2. Max Shachtman, *The Bureaucratic Revolution* (New York: Donald Press, 1962).

3. Myers, *Prophet's Army*, p. 165.

4. Max Shachtman, "Blitzkrieg and Revolution," *New International* 6 (May 1940): 84.

5. *Labor Action*, October 28, 1940.

6. Max Shachtman, "Editor's Comments," *New International* 6 (October 1940): 181.

7. Walter Galenson, *The CIO Challenge to the AFL* (Cambridge, Massachusetts: Harvard University Press, 1960), p. 191.

8. Max Shachtman, "Editor's Comments," *New International* 6 (October 1940): 181; B.J. Widick (Walter Jason), *Labor Action*, August 5, 1940.

9. Max Shachtman, "Labor and Strikes in Wartime," *New International* 7 (April 1941): 39.

10. Ibid, p. 39.

11. Max Shachtman, "Editor's Comments," *New International* 7 (August 1941): 167.

12. *Labor Action*, October 27, 1941.

13. *Labor Action*, August 4, 1941; E.R. McKinney (David Coolidge), *Labor Action*, April 26, 1943.

14. E. R. McKinney, *Labor Action*, August 25, 1941; E.R. McKinney, "The UAW Convention," *New International* 7 (August 1941): 171; E.R. McKinney, *Labor Action*, August 3, 1942.

15. Max Shachtman, *Labor Action*, October 25, 1943.

16. Albert Glotzer (Albert Gates), *Labor Action*, October 4, 1943. Glotzer was a founding member of the CLA, having been expelled from the Communist party as a member of the Cannon–Shachtman group. Theodore Draper, *American Communism and Soviet Russia* (New York: Viking, 1960), p. 372.

17. Max Shachtman, "The Miners Strike and the Labor Party," *New International* 9 (July 1943): 198.

18. Hal Draper, "What Are the Prospects for Socialism," *New International* 9 (July 1943): 224. In fairness to Draper, his criticisms of Shachtman went beyond this one point. Draper rejected the Trotskyist tradition, which had always emphasized the distinction between a "third party" based on individual memberships, and a "labor party" organized around the bloc affiliation of trade unions. Only if the party were a true labor party would working class control over it be ensured, while third parties were often cross-class formations, such as the Farmer–Labor party. Draper argued that with the rise of the CIO any independent party would necessarily be dominated by labor, and thus the previous distinction was no longer a valid one. In the past, an independent party often "arose on the basis of the farmers and lower middle-class predominantly. Today, with the vastly increased social weight of the working class, it can arise only with the labor–liberals standing in their shoes." Hal Draper (Paul Temple), "Ups and Downs of the Party Line on the ALP," *Mimeographia*, 4: 734. Dated Summer 1944. Interestingly enough, Shachtman came over to Draper's position after the Wallace campaign of 1948.

19. Workers Party, "The Fight for a Labor Party," *New International* 9 (December 1943): 330–31.

20. Art Preis, *Labor's Giant Step, Twenty Years of the CIO* (New York: Pioneer, 1964), p. 228.

21. Nelson Lichtenstein, *Labor's War at Home* (Cambridge, England: Cambridge University Press, 1982), pp. 191–96; Irving Howe and B.J. Widick, *The UAW and Walter Reuther* (New York: Random House, 1949), pp. 171, 175.

22. Max Shachtman, *Labor Action*, September 25, 1944.

23. Preis, *Labor's Giant Step*, pp. 243–46; Frank Cormier and William J. Eaton, *Reuther* (Englewood Cliffs, New Jersey: Prentice-Hall, 1970), pp. 212–15.

24. On PAC, see James C. Foster, *The Union Politic* (Columbia: University of Missouri Press, 1975). The head of the CIO at the time was Phillip Murray, also then president of the United Steel Workers. According to David J. McDonald, Murray's closest associate and, in 1943, the secretary-treasurer of the USW, PAC was formed by Murray and the CIO leadership because "talk of forming a Labor Party . . . picked up again in 1943." Thus "when a new move to create an ultraliberal political party in the name of the workingman began to gather steam, Murray and Hillman decided they should counter it with a specific, labor-oriented political action committee that could function within the two-party system." Hillman, the CIO's chief political operative and head of the Amalgamated Clothing Workers, became chair of PAC and McDonald its treasurer. David J. McDonald, *Union Man* (New York: EP Dutton, 1960), p. 169.

25. Herman Benson (Ben Hall), *Labor Action*, March 27, 1944.

26. Max Shachtman, "The PAC, the Elections and the Future," *New International* 10 (October 1944): 308-9.

27. Max Shachtman, "The PAC and the Elections," *New International* 10 (November 1944): 357.

28. Emmanuel Geltman (Emmanuel Garrett), *Labor Action*, March 11, 1946.

29. Lichtenstein, *Labor's War at Home*, p. 695; Cormier and Eaton, *Reuther*, pp. 218-30; Irving Howe and B.J. Widick, *The UAW and Walter Reuther* (New York: Random House, 1949), pp. 132-48.

30. Max Shachtman, "UAW vs. GM," *New International* 11 (December 1945): 260.

31. E.R. McKinney, *Labor Action*, March 25, 1946.

32. Howe and Widick, *UAW and Walter Reuther*, p. 124.

33. Herman Benson, *Labor Action*, March 11, 1946; *Labor Action*, April 22, 1946; E. R. McKinney, *Labor Action*, April 8, 1946.

34. Albert Glotzer, *Labor Action*, August 5, 1946.

35. Emmanuel Geltman, *Labor Action*, September 9, 1946.

36. Max Shachtman, "Circular Letter," *Mimeographia*, 17: 621-22. Dated April 1946.

37. Max Shachtman, *Labor Action*, December 16, 1946.

38. An interesting account from someone who was in a staff position and on the CP side of the 1947 UAW split can be found in Clancy Sigal, *Going Away* (Boston: Houghton, Mifflin, 1961). Also Cormier and Eaton, *Reuther*, pp. 241-54.

39. Max Shachtman, *Labor Action*, December 8, 1947.

40. E.R. McKinney, *Labor Action*, November 10, 1947.

41. E.R. McKinney, *Labor Action*, December 1, 1947.

42. Herman Benson, *Labor Action*, April 31, 1947; Max Shachtman, *Labor Action*, December 8, 1947; B. J. Widick, *Labor Action*, June 30, 1947.

43. Howe and Widick, *UAW and Walter Reuther*, pp. 171, 175.

44. Ibid, p. 175.

45. On the Progressive party, see Curtis MacDougall, *Gideon's Army* (New York: Marzani and Munsell, 1965).

46. Irving Howe (R. Fahan), "What Makes Henry Run?" *New International* 14 (February 1948): 57.

47. UAW Executive Board Minutes, March 3, 1948, pp. 428-31; UAW Executive Board Minutes, September 13, 1948, p. 8, Roy Reuther Archives, Box 2, Walter P. Reuther Library, Wayne State University, Detroit, Michigan. The emphasis from the quote from Walter Reuther is reproduced from the minutes as recorded. Executive board minutes were available to the public. A listing of campaign contributions to liberal Democratic Congressional candidates for the 1948 campaign can also be found in the Roy Reuther Archives.

48. Emmanuel Geltman, *Labor Action*, August 23, 1948. The quotations from the UAW executive board are from the same article.

49. Max Shachtman and Nathan Gould, "The Situation in the United States and Our Tasks," *Mimeographia*, 9: 1874-79. Dated September 1948.

50. Political Committee, "The Situation in the United States and Our Tasks," *Mimeographia*, 9: 2045. For Draper's basic acceptance of a labor party perspective see Hal Draper, "Third Party Trends," *New International* 13 (March 1947): 76-79.

51. Herman Benson, *Labor Action*, January 10, 1949.

52. Shachtman had already proposed that the WP become a looser "propaganda group" in his and Gould's September 1948 internal document. Shachtman and Gould, *Mimeographia*, 9: 1882. Dated September 1948.

53. George Leo Gordon, "Questions on Reuther, the Social Democrat," *Mimeographia*, 8: 1748. Dated March 1948.

54. Gordon Haskell (Larry O'Connor), "A Third Camp Position in the Unions," *Mimeographia*, 9: 1983. Dated December 1949.

55. E.R. McKinney, "Resolution on the Union Question," *Mimeographia*, 10: 2304-5. Dated March 1949.

56. Herman Benson, *Labor Action*, August 8, 1949.

57. Susan Green, "The ISL and Labor Politics," *Mimeographia*, 11: 2431, 2434. Dated April, 1950.

58. Irving Howe and Stanley Plastrik (Henry Judd), "Statement of Resignation," *Mimeographia*, 11: 2538-40. Dated January 1953. Irving Howe, *A Margin of Hope* (New York: Harcourt Brace and Jovanovich, 1982); Michael Harrington and Irving Howe, "Voices from the Left," *New York Times Magazine*, June 17, 1984, pp. 24-28. Howe also helped to found *Dissent* magazine as a forum for social democratic thought in this country.

59. Max Shachtman, *Labor Action*, May 15, 1950.

60. Herman Benson, *Labor Action*, May 15, 1950.

61. Max Shachtman, *Labor Action*, May 27, 1950; Herman Benson, *Labor Action*, May 15, 1950.

62. Saul Berg, *Labor Action*, May 27, 1950.

63. B.J. Widick, *Labor Action*, May 1, 1950.

64. *Labor Action*, July 10, 1950.

65. John Barnard, *Walter Reuther and the Rise of the Auto Workers* (Boston: Little, Brown, 1983), pp. 143-34.

66. Herman Benson, *Labor Action*, April 9, 1951; B.J. Widick, *Labor Action*, September 24, 1951.

67. "Social Forces, Politics in the U.S.," *New International* 17 (July-August 1951): 215-16.

68. Herman Benson, *Labor Action*, April 6, 1953.

69. Political Committee, "Resolution on the Political Situation in the United States," *Mimeographia*, 12: 2615; Max Shachtman, Albert Glotzer, and Gordon Haskell, "Amendment to Resolution," *Mimeographia*, 12: 2616. Dated May 1954.

70. Congress of Industrial Organizations, *Proceedings of the Sixteenth Constitutional Convention* (Washington, D.C.: 1954), p. 486.

71. Gordon Haskell (L.G. Smith), *Labor Action*, December 20, 1954; B. J. Widick, *Labor Action*, December 20, 1954.

72. B.J. Widick, *Labor Action*, June 13, 1955; Herman Benson, *Labor Action*, March 28, 1955.

73. *Labor Action*, June 25, 1956.

74. *Labor Action*, November 5, 1956; Albert Glotzer, "The Case for Socialist Regroupment," *New International* 23 (Spring 1957): 72-74. The Political Committee statement passed by the 1957 ISL convention as the basis for dissolution into the SP can be found in *Mimeographia*, 12: 2671-72.

75. Hal Draper, "The Meaning of Shachtman's 'Socialist Unity,'" *Mimeographia*, 12: 2691. Dated March 1957.

76. Political Committee, "Resolution on Perspectives for American Socialists," *Mimeographia*, 12: 2699. Dated June 1957.

77. Hal Draper and Archie Winters, "Socialists and the Labor Movement," *Mimeographia*, 12: 2747. Dated January 1958.

78. *Labor Action*, June 16, 1958. The SP approved the decision to absorb the ISL at its 1958 convention, but this decision was advisory to a membership referendum. In the summer of 1958, the SP narrowly approved the agreement with the ISL by a vote of 323 to 293. *Socialist Party of America Papers, 1897-1963* (Glen Rock, New Jersey: Microfilming Corporation of America, 1975), Reel 72.

79. *Socialist Party of America Papers*, Reel 71. From a letter by Shachtman to the SP informing the party of the ISL's decision to apply for membership in the SP.

80. *Labor Action*, March 24, 1958.

81. *Labor Action*, June 16, 1958.

10
TWO DECADES OF
REALIGNMENT POLITICS

In 1958, at the time of the ISL's dissolution, the Socialist party was already deeply divided on issues related to electoral politics. The SP had maintained its tradition of electoral independence by running a slate in every presidential election from 1900 through 1956. Yet an increasingly large segment within the party, including Norman Thomas, worked closely with liberals from groups such as the Americans for Democratic Action (ADA). This tendency held that the SP's pretensions to being a viable electoral vehicle only made it more difficult for the SP to be fully accepted within the liberal coalition.[1]

At the 1958 convention, which accepted the ISL's application to join subject to membership referendum, much of the debate focused on the Socialist party's attitude to the Democratic party. The convention resolution, proposed by Norman Thomas, held that "the situation calls for flexibility in the electoral policy of the party." Accordingly, the SP should actively "recruit Democrats or Republicans—or people whose electoral allegiance will remain to those parties." In the same spirit, the SP should permit "actions by individuals in support of labor or avowedly progressive candidates" who are running within the two-party system.[2]

Thus, even before the ISL was absorbed into the SP, the SP had welcomed into membership those committed to reforming the Democratic party. The entry of the Shachtmanites into the SP did not so much alter the overall trend in SP politics as it provided the right wing with a fully developed ideology. This realignment perspective continues to provide the ideological rationale for the entire gamut of leftists whose efforts are directed at transforming the Democratic party and especially for the Democratic Socialists of America (DSA).

The realignment perspective begins with the belief that the Democratic and Republican parties are loose coalitions of interest groups, coalitions that are primarily held together by patronage and not by a shared set of principles. Instead, it is vitally important to create a party that has a coherent set of principles and that consistently represents the interest of working people. Advocates of realignment stress the necessity of building a broad coalition of progressive forces committed to the development of such a party. Up to this point, the analysis coincides with that underlying the labor party perspective, which lay at the core of ISL politics.

Yet from there on the two perspectives fundamentally diverge. Proponents of realignment are convinced that the Democratic party can be transformed into a working class party. In their view, the New Deal was characterized by the strength of the progressive coalition, which began to alter the Democratic party fundamentally in program and structure. The task remains unfinished, which explains the high priority realignment advocates place on recreating a liberal coalition powerful enough to capture again the highest levels of the party structure, thereby ensuring the adoption of a comprehensive program of social reform. Such a victory would spark an exodus of conservatives, primarily southern Dixiecrats, who would then join the Republican party. The result would be a basic realignment of U.S. politics, in which the two major parties would directly reflect basic political differences. Socialists would establish themselves as the loyal leftwing of a realigned Democratic party and the U.S. political scene would come to resemble that found in most Western European countries.

In this scenario, the trade union leadership plays a crucially important role. Only when the official union structure joins with the liberal coalition will it be possible to succeed in transforming the Democratic party. Realignment proponents are convinced that the union hierarchy will be forced to link up with the liberal coalition in order to gain the Democrats' backing for a social program that can defend the gains of the union movement against the increasingly harsh attacks of the rightwing and its corporate allies.

It was former members of the ISL who fully articulated this argument within the Socialist party during the first years of the 1960s. Over this period, Shachtman continued to be the leading ideologue of the group, but he operated increasingly behind the scenes. Instead, Michael Harrington came to the fore as the chief spokesperson for the realignment tendency. At first, Harrington's views were closely in tune with Shachtman's, but the two soon reached an impasse over the war in Vietnam.

Harrington had been a member of the ISL, but he had not played a major role in the ideological debates within that organization. Despite his secondary role in the ISL, most of his formative political experiences came as a protégé of Max Shachtman. Harrington first became prominent in socialist politics as a leader of the youth wing of the Socialist party. In those years, the early 1950s, Harrington's views were those of a radical pacifist. He had worked with the Catholic Worker group in New York and he also claimed conscientious objector status during the Korean War. The SP youth group, the Young People's Socialist League (YPSL), was radicalized by the Korean War, when it opposed U.S. intervention while the majority of the SP supported it. Harrington sympathized with the antiimperialist leftwing of the YPSL, which came to control the organization and which then moved it out of the orbit of the SP and into that of the ISL.[3]

In 1954, the YPSL merged with the youth branch of the ISL to form the Young Socialists League (YSL). Harrington was its chair and, as such, a frequent contributor to ISL publications. His political perspective at the time was very much in the mainstream of the ISL, including his advocacy of independent political action. In a YSL pamphlet on the 1956 elections, Harrington argued that "there is no basic, fundamental difference between the policies of the two major parties." He rejected support for Adlai Stevenson as the lesser evil because "it is not a lesser evil when a party stifles progressive possibilities, when it fails, not our socialist ideals, but its own liberal potentialities." The Michael Harrington of 1956 had no doubts that "there is no way out of this impasse in the Democratic Party. . . . The way out is a labor party."[4]

As with most of those in the ISL, Harrington could hold these unequivocal views on electoral politics, while still agreeing with Shachtman that socialists should avoid antagonizing the labor leadership by running independent candidates against union-endorsed liberals. Furthermore, Harrington supported the ISL's dissolution into the SP, arguing that the differences with the majority, Norman Thomas tendency were "not decisive."[5] From the time the ISL decided to join the SP, Harrington's views underwent a rapid and substantial shift,[6] so that by 1960 Harrington firmly believed in the realignment perspective.

Within the SP, realignment came to the fore at the 1960 convention, which most of those who had been in the ISL could only attend as observers. A key convention resolution called for a fight aiming at "forcing the Dixiecrats out of the Democratic Party." This would result in a "realignment, with conservative forces in one party opposed by a liberal and labor controlled second party."[7]

Soon after the convention, Harrington further delineated the newly adopted perspective in an article commenting on the 1960 elections. The paramount need was "to develop a structure of meaningful political action, to realign American politics," so as to coalesce "a Second Party, one based upon the labor movement, the urban middle-class liberals and progressive farmers."[8]

Harrington went on to repudiate explicitly the central tenet of ISL politics, the imperative necessity of forming a labor party. "For a long time, radicals felt that such a party would develop when the labor movement and other progressive forces left the Democratic Party and raised their own, independent standard.'' Such a perspective seemed hopeful as late as 1948, when Reuther raised the prospect of founding a third party, but "now the likelihood is much greater that realignment will come about through a struggle *within* the Democratic Party."[9]

While Harrington accepted the basic assumptions of realignment politics, he was still disenchanted with most Democratic politicians. He refused to back John Kennedy, stating that "in the 1960 elections, there is no way to vote for change" and that "a vote for John F. Kennedy or Richard Nixon doesn't mean much."[10] This disenchantment with the mainstream of U.S. politics even extended to the labor hierarchy. In late 1961, Harrington remained convinced that "there has been a very real deficiency in effective and aggressive leadership from the AFL-CIO." He even criticized Reuther and the UAW for not acting on their official commitment to realignment. "At their last convention the Auto Workers passed a resolution on political realignment, but, like so many union declarations in recent times, this has remained on the level of a pious hope."[11]

Harrington's adherence to a realignment perspective was matched by Shachtman. In June 1961, Shachtman submitted a resolution to the SP national committee holding that there was an "urgent need for a new political realignment" and that the "SP-SDF is prepared to cooperate with and support all serious forces, both inside and outside the Democratic Party" to bring about such a realignment.[12] Shachtman's resolution was defeated by the national committee, as the majority voted to "reject the concept of subordinating the clear socialist position of the Party to closer collaboration with the official liberal and labor bureaucracy."[13]

During their first years within the SP, the former ISL majority held back from a total acceptance of realignment politics, while accepting the essential premises of that perspective. Nevertheless, their drift to the right was so rapid that, by the time of the 1962 Congressional elections, the Shachtmanites judged the results of these elections solely on the basis of "lesser evil" politics. Over the next two years the position consolidated into a fully developed dogma.

Harrington proposed to the 1962 convention that the SP actively support liberal Democrats in the upcoming elections. In moving toward a political realignment, "the decisive struggle must be waged for the forging of a new progressive liberal–labor political movement in and around the Democratic Party." More immediately, "the Congressional elections offer the chance to elect a small but significant bloc of dedicated champions of peace, civil liberties and economic justice."[14]

In a post mortem on the elections, Harrington argued that "the 1962 elections were a modest step forward," given the gains posted by Congressional liberals. Indeed, he hoped that "they provided the basis for a concerted liberal–labor–radical drive."[15]

By 1964, the former members of the ISL had decided to extend their ties with the union leadership to the top levels of the AFL-CIO. Starting in the late 1940s, ISL members had been active in the Reuther caucus, which had enabled them to establish a considerable credibility within the upper reaches of the UAW hierarchy. With the enthusiastic adoption of a realignment perspective came a more sympathetic stance toward AFL-CIO president George Meany as well as the UAW's Walter Reuther. Contact was made with Lane Kirkland, then secretary-treasurer of the AFL-CIO, through Jack Conway, Reuther's special assistant.[16] Several years later, Harrington defended this move on the basis that "we had determined to be truly radical: to involve ourselves with the leaders elected by the American workers themselves, rather than with those imaginary figures who should have been leading a revolutionary proletariat that did not exist."[17]

In 1963, Harrington became a national figure when his *The Other America*, a journalistic account of poverty in the United States, made the best-seller lists. Shortly afterward, Lyndon Johnson declared a War on Poverty, and Harrington became a government advisor.[18] From his vantage point inside the administration, Harrington fervently defended the administration. He applauded Johnson's landslide victory in 1964 as "the basis for a major period of social change."[19] Harrington was disappointed with the minimal funds available to the poverty program, but he still believed that a fundamental redistribution of income was in the offing. "The broad definition of the Great Society is in keeping with the vision which has inspired every utopian movement of the past, and the socialist movement of the past and present."[20]

Even after Harrington left the administration in protest over the escalation of the war in Vietnam, he still felt that only the war had prevented Johnson from implementing a major program of social reform. "In 1964 I suspect he [Johnson] honestly and genuinely wanted to complete Franklin Roosevelt's New Deal."[21]

VIETNAM AND SOCIALISM

Once inside of the Socialist party, most of the former ISL members quickly jettisoned their previous views. From revolutionary socialists still committed to independent political action, if only hesitantly, they had been transformed by 1964 into proponents of realignment, with links to the AFL-CIO leadership and the Johnson administration. Despite the drastic reversal in political perspective, the ISL cadre remained a remarkably cohesive bloc. All this changed with the war in Vietnam. As the war intensified, the debates within the SP became increasingly divisive, until the disputing factions finally split apart.

At first the debates within the SP pitted a united Shachtman– Harrington tendency against all of those who demanded the immediate withdrawal of U.S. troops from Vietnam. The oppositional group included most of those who had been fighting a rearguard battle against the drift toward the right since 1958, but it also encompassed some of those who had previously been sympathetic to the realignment tendency. David McReynolds, the leading spokesperson for the resurgent leftwing came from this latter group of activists.

McReynolds first became involved in radical politics during the years immediately following World War II, at about the same time as Michael Harrington. He, too, was attracted to pacifist politics, and, indeed, McReynolds has been on the national staff of the War Resisters League for more than 20 years. He first actively participated in socialist politics through the SP youth group, the YPSL, in 1951. In 1954, when most of the YPSL merged with the ISL youth group, McReynolds remained in the Socialist party, but in its leftwing. In 1956, he argued for a labor party perspective, and· he sharply criticized those who wanted to enter the Democratic party. Such a move could only "help [to] destroy any chance of a Labor Party."[22]

McReynolds vocally backed the dissolution of the ISL into the SP. Once the ISL cadre had entered the SP, McReynolds moved in conjunction with them, toward a realignment politics. He voted with the majority of delegates to the 1960 Socialist party convention against running a presidential slate in that year's presidential election, and he also endorsed liberal Democratic candidates in the 1962 elections.[23]

The clearest case of McReynold's acceptance of a realignment perspective can be seen in an article commenting on the 1964 elections. McReynolds was convinced that "the need to vote for Johnson [was] so obvious and imperative" as to require little argument. He extended his support to virtually the entire Democratic slate, holding that socialists should be "voting against every Republican Senator and Congressman who has not broken with Goldwater."[24]

McReynolds was sure that 1964 marked a major step toward a fundamental transformation of the two-party system. "Here is a realignment taking place before our eyes." While the Republicans had been captured by the new Right, the Democrats had nominated Hubert Humphrey for vice-president, and thus at "the Democratic Party Convention we see the same realignment toward a kind of 'Left.'"[25]

Although McReynolds accepted much of the realignment perspective, he was also concerned with the extent to which the Shachtman group was moving rightward and, in particular, with their willingness to downplay socialist politics in order to gain credibility among the top layers of the union leadership. In a letter to the SP national committee, McReynolds wrote "I have increasing doubts about the way in which some comrades interpret the Party's declaration on realignment."[26]

Despite his doubts, McReynolds maintained cordial relations with Shachtman until 1965 and the escalation of the Vietnam War. At its 1964 convention, the SP had condemned U.S. intervention, insisting that "under no circumstances [should the U.S.] continue its investment of men and money in war in Southeast Asia."[27] Following Johnson's decision to escalate the war rapidly in the aftermath of the Tonkin Gulf incident, Martin Oppenheimer, a prominent member of the SP's leftwing, presented a resolution to the national committee demanding "the withdrawal of American men and materials of war from the Vietnam area at once." When the resolution was defeated, McReynolds resigned from the national committee and the battle was joined.[28]

In the first rounds of disputes over the war, the realignment caucus held firmly together. Both Shachtman and Harrington could agree that the United States should press the Saigon government to be less repressive. They were also adamant in their opposition to any call for immediate withdrawal of U.S. troops, in the belief that this would make a National Liberation Front (NLF) victory inevitable, which in turn would lead to the consolidation of a totalitarian regime throughout Vietnam. Finally, they were united in vehemently denouncing the antiwar movement for its militancy and for its inclusion of organizations that uncritically supported the NLF.

The debate within the SP over the Vietnam War can be seen at its clearest in an interchange between Harrington and McReynolds in the *Village Voice* from 1967. McReynolds initiated the discussion with an article in support of the antiwar movement and its militant tactics. He urged leftists from his generation to become more actively involved in the movement, and he specifically urged them to participate in a nonviolent blockade of a New York City induction center organized by the War Resisters League.[29]

Harrington responded by sharply criticizing the politics of the antiwar movement.[30] In order to be effective, "the American anti-war movement must make it politically clear that it is for peace and not for victory for one side or the other." He also rejected the use of militant tactics, in part because they antagonized public opinion. "In my opinion, the rising sentiment against the war has come about in spite of, and not because of, tactics of civil disruption."

Harrington's opposition to militancy went beyond the tactical. He viewed these actions as an attempt to undemocratically coerce the determination of public policy. As long as the U.S. people had the option of affecting governmental decisions through elections, "it is still possible to change policy democratically and nonviolently. Under such circumstances, an elite minority cannot impose its will upon the nation." Harrington specifically rejected McReynolds' proposal to participate in the blockade of an induction center. "It is a responsible tactic to block a door as a witness as long as it is done without any intention of really depriving others of their *civil liberty* to enter a building . . . and quite another thing to 'close down' an induction center."

In his response to Harrington, McReynolds pointed out that both of them bore a moral responsibility for Johnson's actions. Each of them had campaigned "to get as heavy a vote as possible for Johnson" in the belief that the liberal wing of the party "could compel Johnson to embark on a serious program of social reform at home while restraining the military from adventures abroad." Instead, Johnson had escalated the Vietnam War while cutting social service expenditures.[31]

Harrington's commitment to reformism and to the overwhelming importance of the electoral arena as a means of changing state policy led him to criticize sharply the greatest upsurge of militant, radical politics in the postwar period. Even as McReynolds urged socialists to engage in civil disobedience against the war machine, Harrington directed his concern to the potential civil liberty violations incidental to the peaceful disruption of the military apparatus and to a possible right-wing backlash to the militant tactics of the Left.

With the advent of the 1968 presidential campaign, Harrington sought to work for an end to the war through a victory in the Democratic primaries. He also became increasingly scornful of the militant tactics of the antiwar movement, viewing this militancy as a direct threat to the credibility of the liberal–labor coalition within the Democratic party.

At first Harrington backed Eugene McCarthy as the antiwar candidate against Johnson. In his estimation, McCarthy's campaign "did so much more for the cause than the counterproductive gestures of many New Leftists." When Robert Kennedy entered the race, Harrington enthusiastically worked for him. Here was a candidate who could unite the middle-class liberals with black and white workers. Years later, he still believed that Bobby Kennedy "could have changed the course of history."[32]

After Hubert Humphrey won the nomination, Harrington reluctantly backed him. In rationalizing this endorsement, he emphasized the danger of a right-wing backlash to the radicalized antiwar movement. At a time when tens of thousands of people were participating in militant protests and when many activists were being drawn to socialist politics, Harrington was convinced that "there is not the least shred of evidence that 'massive numbers' of Americans are moving to the Left." On the contrary, there was a "terrifying trend to the right in this country." The George Wallace campaign was the cutting edge of this turn to the right, and Harrington expected Wallace to receive 20 percent of the presidential vote. A vote for Humphrey was a vote against Wallace.[33]

Through all of these maneuverings during the 1968 campaign, Harrington consistently attacked every effort at third-party politics. A significant section of the antiwar movement had decided to reject the two-party system and to establish new independent parties. The Peace and Freedom party of California was the most successful of these third parties and as such drew Harrington's ire. "The basic premise underlying the Peace and Freedom tactic is that there is a chasm which separates liberalism and radicalism." But such a strategy went directly counter to the creation of a broad progressive coalition that could even bridge the gap between supporters and opponents of the war. "I want to act so as to promote cooperation now on immediate social issues and between doves and hawks, and thus lay the basis for the coalition of the future."[34]

Harrington's stance during the 1968 election has been examined in considerable detail because 1968 was such a critical year. As the antiwar movement peaked in strength, it opened up genuine alternatives to mainstream U.S. politics. During the 1970s, when the Left was weak and fragmented, Harrington could easily argue that there was no choice but to support the "lesser evil" Democrat. Yet in the 1960s, in the midst of a significant upsurge in activity, Harrington could only denounce the movement for its militancy, as he condemned every effort at independent political action.

THE SP SPLITS

Throughout the first years of the war, the realignment caucus held firmly together in resisting the demands for immediate withdrawal of U.S. troops that were being advanced by the SP's leftwing. The deepening divisions within the SP led McReynolds in 1966 to call for a new caucus, later known as the Debs caucus, for those totally opposed to U.S. intervention in Southeast Asia. At the same time, McReynolds attacked the former members of the ISL. He felt personally betrayed by the maneuverings of the Shachtman group, for whom he had vouched during the bitter dispute over their admission to the SP. "I confess to a sense of bitterness touched with humor at the thought that Max Shachtman, once the ultra-Left purist . . . should now serve as the intellectual rallying point for the most extreme elements in the Party's right-wing."[35]

For those on its leftwing, the SP's continued support for the war and the endorsement of Hubert Humphrey by its leadership were acutely disquieting. By March 1969, McReynolds wrote that he did "not consider Shachtman's group . . . either democratic or socialist, let alone comrades." Soon afterward, he resigned from the SP, although most of those in the Debs caucus continued to struggle within the party.[36]

The same period saw the first indications of a major breach within the realignment caucus. From the time Johnson escalated the war, tensions had increased between Shachtman and Harrington. Shachtman in essence gave critical support to the U.S. occupation of South Vietnam as the lesser evil alternative to a communist victory. Harrington refused to back either side, while opposing a further escalation that could only result in a diversion of funds from social services as it deepened the fissures within the liberal–labor coalition.

Until 1970, these tensions within the realignment caucus remained submerged as the caucus attacked the leftwing for advocating immediate withdrawal. Finally, Harrington accepted the need for a unilateral, phased withdrawal of U.S. troops, and the previously cohesive group of former ISL members began to disintegrate. At the June 1970 convention of the SP, the realignment caucus had patched together a compromise resolution, which they passed over the objections of the Debs caucus. According to the resolution, "America must now commit itself to a cease-fire and speedy disengagement from Vietnam. The pace, but not the fact, of our leaving should depend on whether the Thieu-Ky regime begins to implement a program of genuine democratization." This section reflected Harrington's views, but the resolution went on to insist that "all other *foreign* troops must be withdrawn from South Vietnam . . . especially those of North Vietnam" and that "strong political pressure must be brought to bear on the North Vietnamese to respond to American troop withdrawal with corresponding de-escalation of their own."[37]

Shachtman refused to accept the compromises contained in the 1970 resolution, and the underlying divisions soon led to a collision. Shachtman denounced the call for a phased unilateral withdrawal since this would be an "open invitation to Hanoi . . . to consummate its imperial and totalitarian objectives in South Vietnam." Given the choice of a communist victory or the Saigon regime, the United States should continue to give "aid and training, economic and military," to the Saigon regime so that "the South Vietnamese are in a better position to pursue their own defense."[38]

Shachtman developed a comprehensive rationale for his critical support for the war. He recognized that Vietnam was being torn apart by a civil war, but he insisted that the regime of General Thieu represented a better choice than the National Liberation Front. "Communist victory . . . would wipe out all possibilities for democratic development in the country. A non-Communist South Vietnam, even under the Saigon regime, still leaves intact . . . if only embryonically, a variety of social and political forces that are independent of both the Saigon government and totalitarianism."

Shachtman's argument in this passage is remarkably similar to arguments made later by conservative ideologues such as Jeanne Kirkpatrick, President Reagan's first ambassador to the United Nations.

According to this viewpoint, no matter how corrupt or dictatorial a U.S. client state might be, these "authoritarian" regimes are bound to allow more scope for a democratic opposition than is the case in "totalitarian" communist regimes.

While recognizing the "roots in Vietnamese history" of the current conflict, Shachtman nevertheless argued that "the war in Vietnam . . . is above all dominated by the Cold War." Here, in the battle between capitalism and communism, he voiced a "socialist preference" for capitalism. "Under capitalism as it exists in the most advanced countries there are extensive possibilities for expanding the wide degree of political democracy that already exists. Under Communism a totalitarian despotism viciously exploits the people economically and smashes all their democratic rights and movements." Furthermore, in protecting its global interests, "Washington is frequently obliged to maintain and strengthen democratic forces—or at least the conditions which these forces require to develop and grow." Just as had happened in Europe and Japan after World War II, when the United States "established or restored political democracy and progressive social reforms," the United States "to a considerable extent finds itself obliged to follow a similar course in Vietnam." Shachtman's analysis represents the logical underpinnings of a perspective that led him into the rightwing of the Democratic party and that continues to guide his followers in the Social Democrats, USA.

In responding to Shachtman's argument, Harrington accepted most of the underlying logic without accepting the resulting policy implications for Vietnam.[39] Although "it is absolutely true to say that we 'prefer' political democracy, even bourgeois democracy, to totalitarianism," it does not follow "that whenever there is a conflict between bourgeois democratic regimes and Communist regimes or movements we always support the former." Because the capitalist powers tend "to ally [themselves] with feudalists, reactionaries, oligarchs [and] dictators," they often create "situations where politically democratic countries conduct an 'anti-Communist' struggle in such a way as to promote the victory of Communism."

Harrington's answer to Shachtman was an extremely pragmatic one. United States intervention in Vietnam should be opposed because it is a failure, even in its own terms. By backing the corrupt Thieu-Ky regime, the United States had become enmeshed in a "savage, unwinnable and indeterminate war." In "opposing Communism with reactionary anti-Communism," the United States has only "rendered an eventual Communist victory more likely."

The increasingly acrimonious debate over the war provided the basis for a final series of splits within the Socialist party. In November 1971, Harrington formed a new caucus, a caucus that was to become the core of the Democratic Socialist Organizing Committee (DSOC).[40] With him from the start were such other key members of the Young Socialist League from the 1950s as Deborah Meier and Bogdan Denitch, as well as such long-time ISL activists as Gordon Haskell and B.J. Widick.

By the time of the SP convention in March 1972, many of those opposed to the war had quit the party, enabling the Shachtman tendency to pass another resolution giving critical support to the Vietnam War. This led those who remained in the Debs caucus to quit as a group. Their statement of resignation condemned the SP for its stance on the war and called for the immediate withdrawal of U.S. troops from Southeast Asia. The statement also attacked the SP majority for its uncritical support for Democratic candidates, and it counterposed the need for independent political action, even as it allowed that "some of us are for supporting left-liberal Democrats."[41]

With the left wing gone, Harrington's group became the primary target for attacks from the majority tendency. The split finally occurred around the McGovern campaign. Harrington had first endorsed Edmund Muskie in the 1972 Democratic presidential primary, but after Muskie withdrew he backed George McGovern. "The crucial task of the democratic Left in this election year is to help build a vast coalition to oust Richard Nixon," and on this basis "McGovern is best qualified to lead the Democratic ticket next November."[42]

While Harrington urged the SP to jump on the McGovern bandwagon, those in the majority tendency held back. They were deeply suspicious of McGovern's antiwar supporters, and they were worried that McGovern himself would not take a sufficiently hard line toward the communist bloc countries. Their critical stance also reflected the views of the AFL-CIO leadership, which refused to endorse McGovern even after he became the Democratic nominee.

As loyal Democrats, the SP majority supported McGovern after the Democratic convention but with little enthusiasm and a great deal of unconcealed bitterness. The official SP position held that the party "prefers a victory" for the Democratic nominee, but it also explicitly stated that its "members who feel that they cannot support McGovern are of course free to hold and express this view publicly." McGovern's foreign policy statements struck a sensitive nerve with the Shachtman tendency. According to the SP's election statement, McGovern's views on these issues "run contrary to what is required to build a new America in a free world." Indeed, the SP newspaper, *New America*, held that the candidates' proposals to cut the military budget "would make it impossible for the United States to maintain its present defense commitments."[43]

In October 1972, Harrington publicly resigned as cochair of the SP, and the split was complete. He condemned the SP for coming "to so identify itself with the Meany wing of the labor movement that it so supports it even when, as in the case of AFL-CIO neutrality in the 1972 election, it is wrong.'' This blind attachment to Meany and the AFL-CIO hierarchy had prevented the SP from understanding that *"the* priority of the democratic Left" in 1972 was the defeat of Nixon.[44]

By February 1973, Harrington's caucus had reorganized itself as the Democratic Socialist Organizing Committee (DSOC), and it had begun its drive to become the focal point for realignment politics. Shachtman died in November 1972, and a month later his tendency dropped the name Socialist party and became the Social Democrats, USA. This group continues to be closely tied to the AFL-CIO leadership and to Albert Shanker of the American Federation of Teachers (AFT). The name change left the former Debs caucus free to reform the Socialist party in May 1973. Thus the three-way division within the SP during the 1960s has become crystallized into three different organizations, each of which continues to occupy the same position in the political spectrum today.[45]

DSOC AND THE LIBERAL COALITION

Over the last decade, the DSOC has become the largest organization on the Left. The Democratic Socialist Organizing Committee was renamed the Democratic Socialists of America (DSA) in 1982 after merging with the majority tendency of the New American Movement (NAM).[46] In its founding statement, DSOC announced its commitment to a realignment perspective. Despite "the unprincipled and unprogrammatic character of the American party system," the new organization intended to act "as part of the left wing of the Democratic Party, in order to change this party itself, to turn it into a new kind of mass party."[47]

Since then the organization has avidly pursued this goal, primarily by working through the Democratic Agenda, a loose coalition of liberals acting as a caucus within the Democratic party. It has also consolidated its ties with the more progressive elements within the union hierarchy, especially with the top ranks of the UAW and the American Federation of State, County and Municipal Employees (AFSCME).

Throughout its history, Michael Harrington has been DSOC's and now DSA's leading spokesperson and ideologue. Over the decade, Harrington's stance has remained remarkably consistent despite the rightward drift in the domestic political terrain. He remains a loyal Democrat who is convinced that the party can be transformed by the liberal–labor coalition. In conjunction with this bedrock belief in the prospects for realignment, Harrington has consistently stressed the potential for fundamental reform within the constraints of U.S. capitalism.

Harrington's views on U.S. imperialism provide a clear example of his belief in the potential for a thoroughgoing reform of U.S. society. In the early 1970s, at a time of pervasive disillusionment with U.S. foreign policy, Harrington sought to convince other socialists that imperialism was not intrinsically linked to the capitalist social system of this country. He insisted that the antiwar movement "must assert that it is possible for the U.S. to act democratically and peacefully within the world under the auspices of a principled liberal administration."[48]

Ten years later, the United States was once again rebuilding its military power in order to defend its global strategic and economic interests. The escalating arms race again became a flashpoint for resistance, and again Harrington directed his efforts to restraining radical visionaries. He has expressed concern that those on the Left are insufficiently sensitive to the Soviet military threat. "It would be wrong for the left to talk as if the national security of this country is not a matter of concern, or is something that can be easily achieved." In order to avoid projecting such a harmful impression, the "democratic left has the difficult task of . . . putting forth proposals for a lean defense system that meets the needs of the national security of the United States." Although Harrington has endorsed efforts to block the installation of new cruise missiles in Western Europe, he remains convinced that those in the peace movement who propose that the United States should dismantle a significant proportion of its enormous stockpile of nuclear bombs and missiles are being "politically irresponsible."[49]

Harrington and DSA have also been uncritical enthusiasts of the "progressive" wing of the labor hierarchy. Jerry Wurf, the long-time president of the AFSCME, died in 1983 and was eulogized in the organization's newsletter as "a socialist from 1935 until his death." Wurf had systematically extended the power of the national officers at the expense of the autonomy of union locals. Harrington's ties to the UAW leadership remain close. He has extolled UAW president Owen Bieber for being "excellent on foreign policy issues" and for demonstrating "a quality of informed passion" on the problems confronting U.S. workers.[50]

Efforts to win the confidence of the union hierarchy have been extended to even the more conservative of the elite. In his 1972 book, *Socialism*, Harrington wrote that George Meany, then AFL-CIO president, had "the same outlook as the European social democracy." As evidence for this unlikely statement, Harrington pointed to testimony before a Congressional hearing. Meany responded to a question as to whether he was a socialist by granting that he believed that working people should receive "a better share of whatever wealth the economy produces," and thus "if that is socialism then I guess I am a socialist." Of course, Meany went on to say that he did not consider himself to be a socialist.[51]

A decade later, Harrington still held out hope for the AFL-CIO hierarchy, only it was Lane Kirkland who then held Meany's post and won Harrington's praise. "There has been a significant, and on the whole progressive, shift in the AFL-CIO under Lane Kirkland's leadership."[52]

Harrington's links to the union bureaucracy run so deep that they hinder his efforts to reform the Democratic party. The Democratic Socialist Organizing Committee initiated the Democratic Agenda as an organizational framework for its attempts to coalesce a liberal pressure group within the party. In 1978, the Agenda was able to use the midterm convention as a forum to pressure the Carter administration to adopt more liberal policies. Four years later, the Democratic leadership carefully manipulated the entire event in order to ensure a monolithic unity behind a moderate program. The party leaders relied on the support of a large caucus of trade union delegates to steamroller the convention successfully.[53]

Although Harrington was unhappy with the stifling of debate at the conference, he still viewed the AFL-CIO's decision to participate more actively in Democratic party politics as "a progressive organizational development" in which "workers identify themselves in politics on a class basis."[54] Harrington is caught in an insoluble bind. He supports the liberal reformers within the party, but he is also tied to the union leadership that has been instrumental in silencing every challenge to the Democratic party hierarchy and its establishment politics.

Needless to say, Harrington remains firmly convinced that the Democratic party is the primary arena in which progressive forces can bring about fundamental social change. In 1976, he backed Jimmy Carter, one of the most conservative Democratic presidential nominees in the history of that party, as "clearly and infinitely better than Gerald Ford."[55] More recently, a Harrington-written DSOC resolution described Teddy Kennedy as "the most effective national politician" in the United States who was "infinitely preferable to Carter." Indeed, according to the resolution, Kennedy's 1980 presidential campaign offered "the democratic Left the greatest opportunity since the era of the New Deal, and the socialist component of that democratic Left the most important opening in half a century."[56]

When Kennedy was defeated by Carter for the 1980 nomination, the DSOC national committee prohibited the organization's spokespeople from publicly backing Carter, and at the same time it enjoined local chapters from working for Barry Commoner, the Citizens Party candidate. Harrington still made it known that he personally supported Carter as the less objectionable of the two major candidates.[57]

During the course of the 1984 elections, DSA has moved even further into the mainstream. Over the latter stages of the primaries, all three of the Democratic aspirants gained significant support within the organization. For Manning Marable, black scholar and DSA vice-chair, Jesse Jackson was "the most left-wing candidate for the presidency since Norman Thomas." Still other influential DSA members backed Mondale as a liberal and the candidate of labor. There were even a few members of the DSA, such as Mike Rotkin, a former NAM activist, who supported Senator Hart as the most electable of the three candidates.[58]

Predictably, once Mondale was nominated, DSA rallied quickly behind him. Its National Committee lauded the Mondale–Ferraro slate as "infinitely superior to Ronald Reagan on every count." Although Mondale was warned that "politics as usual will not defeat Ronald Reagan" and that it was critically important to transform the campaign into "a grassroots movement of the people with a new vision of America," the organization nevertheless vowed to "vigorously back, and work for" the Democratic ticket.[59]

The Democratic Socialists of America no longer stands for a program committed to the total restructuring of the Democratic party. Indeed, its response to the 1984 Democratic primaries demonstrated all too clearly the extent to which differences within DSA reflect the broad spectrum of opinion within the Democratic party itself and not just the party's left wing. Realignment politics has been diluted into little more than bland generalities and pious hopes.

CONCLUSIONS

Once the ISL dissolved into the SP, the Shachtmanites quickly cut the last ties to their pasts as revolutionary socialists. At the core of this political disintegration was a corrosive cynicism. After many years in and around the labor movement, the ISL cadre had completely lost its confidence in the strength and militancy of the working class. With the acceptance of a deep-seated pessimism went any commitment to a socialist politics beyond the fond hope for a better future society.

Instead, the former members of the ISL came to identify union officials as the authentic representatives of the working class. For Shachtman and those who followed him to the end, this new perspective led to an alliance with George Meany and Albert Shanker, the most conservative elements in the AFL-CIO bureaucracy.[60] To Harrington and DSA, only the more progressive wing of the union leadership can be unconditionally supported. These differing allegiances correspond to a split among the former ISL cadres in their attitude toward U.S. military intervention in the Third World and toward the current escalation in the arms race.

While Shachtman and the Social Democrats, USA severed any contact with the radical movement, Harrington and DSA continue to occupy a middle ground. Their policies remain oriented toward implementing a program of social reform within the limits of a capitalist system. Winning such a program requires the creation of a strong liberal–labor coalition within the Democratic party, so that liberal candidates can become the Democratic standard bearers.

Yet the record of the last 20 years demonstrates that the realignment perspective is a failure in its own terms. Over this period, the mainstream of the Democrats has shifted significantly rightward. The hard-won victories of the McGovern campaign, which had led to a certain openness in the party's structure, have been reversed without a fight.[61] Currently, DSA finds itself without any meaningful influence within the power centers of the Democratic party as it seeks to adapt its policies to those of its patrons in the trade union bureaucracy.

Not only has realignment been a failure in terms of transforming the Democratic party, but a perspective that emphasizes political maneuvers within the higher circles of the liberal coalition is bound to blunt any commitment to radical insurgencies. For realignment advocates, social progress is primarily measured by legislative victories. This places a premium on skillful politicking within the official structures, governmental and nongovernmental, and not on building a mass movement. On the contrary, an upsurge in militant activity becomes a threat to the carefully worked out arrangements of well-connected liberal leaders. Harrington's role in the 1960s, when he acted as a hostile critic of the antiwar movement, cannot be understood as a personal idiosyncracy, but rather it represents a logical extension of the realignment perspective.

Harrington has defended his political perspective as the "left-wing of the possible" and yet the record decisively demonstrates that realignment is neither left-wing nor possible.[62]

SOURCES

In studying the Socialist Party from 1958 through 1972, I have relied heavily on the party's archives, which are located at Duke University. They are microfilmed as *The Socialist Party of America Papers, 1877–1963* (Glen Rock, New Jersey: Microfilming Corporation of America, 1975) and as *The Socialist Party of America Papers, 1919–1976 Addendum* (Glen Rock, New Jersey: Microfilming Corporation of America, 1977).

NOTES

1. Norman Thomas urged the SP to drop its own independent electoral campaigns in 1950. He saw the SP as playing a role similar to that of the British Fabians for those involved in progressive movements and within the liberal wing of the Democratic party. Murray B. Seidler,

Norman Thomas: *The Respectable Rebel* (Syracuse, New York: Syracuse University Press, 1961), p. 235.

2. *Socialist Party, Addendum*, Reel 9.

3. *Time*, February 7, 1964, p. 25; Michael Harrington, *Fragments of a Century* (New York: EP Dutton, 1973). Harrington joined the Catholic Worker in 1950 and the YPSL in the following year.

4. Michael Harrington, "What Choice for Youth in the Elections," *Independent Socialist Mimeographia* (Berkeley, California: Independent Socialist Press, 1971), 28: 256-57.

5. *Labor Action*, May 27, 1957. From the statement of the YSL national executive board supporting merger with the SP.

6. Already in the fall of 1957 Harrington held that a fundamental "realignment" in U.S. politics was essential, a realignment that could occur either through the formation of an independent party or "through a fight within the Democratic party leading . . . to the expulsion of the South and the victory of the labor movement." *Labor Action*, October 7, 1957.

7. *Socialist Party Papers, Addendum*, Reel 10.

8. The following quotes are from Michael Harrington, "1960 Elections Predicted," *Liberation* 5 (October 1960): 11.

9. Ibid, p. 12.

10. Michael Harrington, "After the Union Ball," *Commonweal* 75 (November 3, 1961): 143, 146.

11. *Socialist Party Papers, Addendum*, Reel 8.

12. Hammer and Tongs (1962: 1), *Socialist Party Papers,* Reel 129.

13. *Socialist Party Papers, Addendum*, Reel 10.

14. *New America*, December 3, 1962. In fact, the Democrats did very well in the 1962 Congressional elections, considering that they were the incumbent party in an off-year election. The Democrats gained three seats in the Senate and maintained a large majority in the House with minimal losses.

15. *New America*, December 3, 1962.

16. Harrington, *Fragments of a Century*, p. 192.

17. Ibid, p. 198.

18. *Time*, February 7, 1964, p. 25; Harrington, *Fragments of a Century*, p. 174; Michael Harrington, *The Other America: Poverty in the United States* (New York: Macmillan, 1962).

19. *New America*, November 16, 1964.

20. *New America*, January 18, 1965.

21. Michael Harrington, "Voting the Lesser Evil," *Commentary* 45 (April 1968): 24.

22. Hammer and Tongs (1965:2), *Socialist Party Papers*, Reel 129; Hammer and Tongs (1956: ?), *Socialist Party Papers*, Reel 129.

23. *New York Times*, October 12, 1980; *Socialist Party Papers, Addendum*, Reel 10; *Socialist Party Papers, Addendum*, Reel 8.

24. David McReynolds, "The Election: A Referendum," *Liberation* 9 (October 1964): 4, 24.

25. Ibid, p. 26.

26. *Socialist Party Papers, Addendum*, Reel 8. The reference is to the SP's 1960 resolution on realignment cited in Note 7.

27. Hammer and Tongs (1965: 2), *Socialist Party Papers*, Reel 129.

28. Ibid; *Socialist Party Papers, Addendum*, Reel 37.

29. *Village Voice*, November 30, 1967.

30. The following quotes are from *Village Voice*, December 7, 1967. The emphasis in the quote two paragraphs following is mine.

31. *Village Voice*, December 21, 1967.

32. Michael Harrington, "Letters," *Commentary* 46 (July 1968): 17; Harrington, *Fragments of a Century*, p. 214.

33. *New America*, September 30, 1968. Wallace actually received 13 percent of the vote and soon faded from the national scene.

34. Michael Harrington, "Voting the Lesser Evil," *Commentary* 45 (April 1968): 26.

35. *Socialist Party Papers*, Reel 129.

36. *Socialist Party Papers, Addendum*, Reel 13.

37. Hammer and Tongs, "Resolution on Southeast Asia" (October 9, 1970), *Socialists Party Papers, Addendum*, Reel 129. The emphasis is mine.

38. The following quotes are from Hammer and Tongs, "Statement on Vietnam" (October 9, 1970), *Socialist Party Papers, Addendum*, Reel 129. The statement is signed by Max Shachtman and seven leading members of his tendency. A strikingly similar perspective is presented in Jeanne Kirkpatrick, *Dictatorships and Double Standards* (New York: Simon And Schuster, 1982), pp. 23-51.

39. Michael Harrington, "Socialists and Reactionary Anti-Communism," Hammer and Tongs (October 9, 1970), *Socialists Party Papers, Addendum*, Reel 129.

40. *Socialist Party Papers, Addendum*, Reel 9.

41. *Socialist Party Papers, Addendum*, Reel 9.

42. *Socialist Party Papers, Addendum*, Reel 8.

43. *New America*, September 30, 1968; *New America*, July 31, 1968. For the AFL-CIO's statement of neutrality see *The New York Times*, July 20, 1972.

44. Michael Harrington, "A Call to American Socialists," *The Nation* 215 (November 13, 1972): 1455. The emphasis is Harrington's. Harrington submitted his resignation from the SP, by then renamed the Social Democrats, USA, in June 1973. *New America*, July 20, 1973.

45. Harrington, *Fragments of a Century*, p. 245; *New America*, December 31, 1972; *Socialist Party of America Papers, 1919-1976, Addendum: A Guide to the Microfilm Edition* ed. Elizabeth H. Murphey (Glen Rock, New Jersey: Microfilming Corporation of America, 1972), p. 2.

46. Sandra Chelnov, "DSOC/NAM = DSA," *Democratic Left* 10 (March 1982): 5.

47. Democratic Socialist Organizing Committee, *We Are Socialists of the Democratic Left* (October 1973).

48. Michael Harrington, "Prospects for a Peace Movement," *The Nation* 216 (June 11, 1973): 742.

49. Michael Harrington, "Finding a Defense Balance," *Democratic Left* 9 (November 1981): 6.

50. Harry Fleischman, "On the Left," *Democratic Left* 10 (March 1982), p. 15; Michael Harrington, "Organizer's Diary," *Democratic Left* 12 (March-April 1984): 11.

51. Michael Harrington, *Socialism* (New York: Saturday Review, 1972), p. 268.

52. Michael Harrington, "Toward Solidarity Day II," *Democratic Left* 10 (September-October 1982): 3.

53. "Democratic Agenda," *Democratic Left* 7 (February 1979): 7; *New York Times*, June 27-29, 1982.

54. Harrington, "Toward Solidarity Day II," p. 4.

55. Peter Camejo and Michael Harrington, *The Lesser Evil* (New York: Pathfinder Press, 1977), p. 11.

56. Michael Harrington, *Draft Resolution on 1980 Election Policy*. Typescript. Passed with minor modifications by the DSOC national board in October 1979 as organizational policy. The gist of the statement can be found in *Democratic Left* 8 (February 1980): 6.

57. The essence of DSOC's position in the final round of the elections is contained in "DSOC Resolution on the 1980 Elections," *Democratic Left* 8 (October 1980): 2.

58. Manning Marable, "Why Stick with Jesse," *Democratic Left* 12 (January-February 1984): 8-9; *Guardian*, April 18, 1984.

59. "Presidential Support Statement," *Democratic Left* 12 (July-August 1984): 3.

60. Shachtman became a confidential advisor to Albert Shanker, the head of the American Federation of Teachers. Shanker also retained Shachtman's wife as an

administrative assistant. Albert Glotzer, "Max Shachtman—A Political-Biographical Essay," *Bullentin of the Tamiment Institute* (April 1983): 7. Shachtman's followers have continued on this path. Penn Kemble, who joined Shachtman in signing the internal SP statement in support of the Vietnam War, went on to be an advisor to the AFL-CIO leadership. He is now a key political strategist for the Institute on Religion and Democracy. This "institute" devotes itself to assailing the National Council of Churches for aiding left-wing insurgencies in Third World countries. *New York Times*, February 16, 1983.

61. Thomas J. Reese, "Presidential Nominations: A Process Reformed Again," *America* 146 (May 1, 1982): 34–42. I have analyzed the failures of the realignment strategy more fully in "Revolutionary Socialists and Independent Political Action," *Against the Current* 2 (Winter 1982): 33–37.

62. Harrington frequently uses this phrase to describe his own and DSA's politics. For instance, see "1980 and Beyond: The DSOC and the Left," *Socialist Review* 9 (July–August 1979): 15–50.

PART IV
A SUMMING UP

11
FOR AN INDEPENDENT POLITICS

From the midnineteenth century, most socialists have been convinced that the working class needs its own party, distinct from the already existing political parties. In most European countries, the industrial revolution created a workforce that first fought for the right to vote and then used the franchise to support its own independent party. Before World War I, when socialists felt part of an irresistible and rapidly growing wave, virtually every tendency within the international socialist movement advocated independent political action and criticized those few leftists such as the Fabians who urged the permeation of the established parties.

Working class parties became a major electoral force in most European countries within a few decades of the onset of industrialization. Britain appeared to be an exception to this general rule until the 1890s, when a series of bitter strikes led to an upsurge in industrial unionism. After that, the drive toward an independent politics gathered momentum until the formation of the Labour party in 1900. By the end of World War I, Labour had supplanted the Liberals as the leading electoral alternative to the Conservatives.

The United States remains as the one advanced capitalist country in which a left-wing independent party has never been able to break definitively through the constraints of the two-party system. Only the Socialist party at the turn of the century was able to project itself as a mass party by bringing together a wide spectrum of positions on the Left into one organization. At its zenith in 1912, the SP attracted nearly a million votes, enrolled 100,000 members, and elected several of its candidates to state legislatures, and even to Congress. To avoid being coopted, the party zealously guarded its independence from the two establishment parties. Despite its initial success, the SP could not retain its popular support in the face of the tide of jingoism unleashed by World War I and the coordinated campaign of government repression that followed. Weakened by these attacks, the SP was shattered by the Russian Revolution and the founding of the Communist party.

Since the decline of the SP as a mass party, no other radical party has been able to sustain a significant electoral presence. Successive generations of socialists have become discouraged by the limited success of independent political campaigns, and, in their frustration, many have opted to moderate their views in order to work within the liberal wing of the Democratic party. This trend has been accentuated since the 1930s and the New Deal. For the first time, organized labor and the black community were brought into the Democratic party on an ongoing basis. Since then, socialists who reject independent political action as inappropriate to the United States have sometimes defended their position as being in accord with that of most working people, so that, from this perspective, any other position is intrinsically elitist and dogmatic.

Needless to say, leftists throughout the world have often found themselves in a small minority. In the 1890s, when British socialists were instrumental in organizing the first independent campaigns, most workers consistently voted for the Liberals. More recently in this country, those who opposed the Vietnam War from the start did so despite Johnson's popularity and the widespread support for his tough stand. In both of these cases, a majority of working people soon came to agree with the dissident minority. The important question is not the current popularity of a strategic option, but whether its adoption would facilitate the development of a mass movement in opposition to the existing system.

A more serious argument for a realignment perspective stresses the exceptional circumstances that characterize the U.S. political scene. In particular, the specifics of the electoral process, plurality elections, and the direct election of a president are frequently cited as obstacles that make the formation of a viable third party a virtual impossibility.[1]

The experience of the Socialist party in its heyday before World War I demonstrates the limitations of this argument. From 1900 to 1912, the SP steadily increased its share of the total vote at the Congressional level, even though the party was consistently underrepresented in Congress because of the bias inherent in plurality elections. Furthermore, Eugene Debs ran slightly ahead of the SP's Congressional slate in each of his presidential campaigns over this period.[2] The Socialist party gained in strength because its voters were convinced that the party presented a political alternative that was qualitatively different from, and far preferable to, that offered by the two established parties. Nor can the party's underrepresentation in legislative bodies account for its decline. On the contrary, those in power consciously used the hysteria generated by World War I to eliminate a potentially dangerous opposition through a concerted campaign of repression.

The origin of the United States as a frontier society is often held to be a key factor explaining the continued dominance of the two-party system. Certainly mass working class parties were quickly formed in those countries that experienced rapid industrialization and that were emerging from a rigid feudal tradition. Germany presents a classic example of this interaction. Still, Canada, the country most similar to the United States, was another frontier society, and also one in which socialist politics was slow to develop a popular base. Only during the Great Depression of the 1930s, well after the first stages of industrialization, did Canadian workers and farmers succeed in founding the Cooperative Commonwealth Federation (CCF), now the New Democratic Party.

One factor that has been crucial in precluding the formation of a mass working class party has been this country's enormous social and ethnic diversity. The United States has received wave after wave of immigrants, including of people with a variety of cultural backgrounds and speaking an assortment of different languages. Building a unified and coherent class consicousness within such a diverse population is extremely difficult. Nevertheless, by itself this factor should not provide an insurmountable barrier. The Canadian prairies of the 1930s, an area where the CCF quickly gained a mass base of support, was inhabited by an ethnically diverse population, which was deeply split by religious belief.[3] For the Socialist party at the turn of the century, the problem was even more acute. The SP succeeded in recruiting immigrants from a wide variety of backgrounds by creating autonomous language federations.[4] In contrast to that period, the United States no longer consists of a population of first-generation immigrants, and English is spoken by the great majority of working people.

An even greater obstacle to class consciousness has been the ideological impact of the U.S. role as a world power. Most workers believe that the military defense of U.S. strategic and economic interests is directly congruent with their own well-being. Chauvinism is deeply rooted in U.S. history. Patrotic fever engendered by World War I provided the context in which the Socialist party could be destroyed as a mass party. During World War II, the most radical formations to come out of the tumultuous years of the Great Depression—the CIO unions and the farmer–labor parties of the prairie states—were coopted into the political mainstream.

Since the Vietnam War, the United States no longer has the aura of invincibility. Room is being created for a politics that challenges the interventionist policies perpetuated by the Democratic and Republican parties. The decline of the U.S. empire, along with continuing economic stagnation, may well be providing the objective basis, over the long-run, for the formation of an independent party that can become a significant electoral force.

In any case, whatever the explanation, no party has succeeded in solidifying a popular constituency since the glory days of the Socialist party. In the light of this fact, many socialist have decided that only a strategy aimed at reforming the Democratic party is practical. Yet these efforts have also met with failure. The Democratic party is more conservative and more bureaucratic than it was 50 years ago. Realignment politics has proven to be no more "practical," in the sense of short-run success, than independent political action. Does this mean that the choice between these two strategies is inconsequential, merely a preference between two failed policies?

On the contrary, the decision to work within the Democratic party is almost always linked to a major shift in world-view. Realignment advocates wind up downplaying a radical critique of the existing system, most especially as it relates to corporate liberals. Given the enormous difficulties in winning structural reforms, socialists from this tendency tend to magnify every small gain and ignore the many defeats.

Of course strategic analysis has a direct impact on political practice. For those working within the Democratic party, the need to retain the confidence of influential liberals leads to an enormous distrust of grass-roots militancy. Social movements are inherently destablizing to the status quo and thus threatening to the standing of those in power, whether liberals or conservatives. As a consequence, each period of intensive activism creates the anomolous situation in which socialists aligned with the Democratic party chastise movement activists for being too militant. Often advocates of realignment direct their fire at revolutionary socialists who remain outside of the two-party system and who are spurring these social movements to adopt a more consistently radical position.

In the case of the Communist party during the late 1930s, once inside the New Deal coalition, the party soon became convinced that a fundamental realignment was already in progress. An alliance of progressive forces, the Popular Front, was gaining in power within the Democratic party, leading conservative Democrats to switch parties and become Republicans. Despite this rosy prognosis, the Democratic party drifted rightward after the 1930s, as the trade union movement lost its militancy and became coopted into the mainstream. One feature of this rightward drift was the exacerbation of Cold War tensions in the aftermath of World War II and the exclusion of the CP from the liberal coalition.

During the Popular Front years, the CP used its influence within the CIO unions and, in particular, the UAW to promote its standing within the New Deal coalition. Increasingly, a militant trade union movement became an embarrassment to the CP leadership. At key moments Communist cadre in the UAW were ordered to contain wildcat strikes and to avoid any confrontation with the auto corporations.

In contrast to the Communist party, the Trotskyists, who refused to enter the Democratic party, developed an incisive critique of the New Deal. Without obscuring the critical distinction between fascism and bourgeois democracy, Trotskyist theoreticians examined the role of the Roosevelt administration as a coordinator and stabilizer of a capitalist system on the verge of economic collapse. In the UAW of the 1930s, Trotskyists joined with Socialist party activists in support of a militant struggle to extend shop-floor control over the pace of production. During World War II, cadre from the Workers party were instrumental in organizing the Rank and File caucus in the UAW, while the Communist party denounced every unauthorized strike as a treacherous blow to the war effort.

This same dichotomy can be traced through the events of the 1960s. By that time, the Socialist party was led by members of the Shachtman tendency, who had become fervent advocates of working within the Democratic party. For Michael Harrington and his circle, who were later to constitute the nucleus of the Democratic Socialists of America, the Vietnam War posed a real quandary. The enthusiasm for the Johnson administration and its domestic policies clashed with their opposition to the U.S. military escalation in Southeast Asia.

Harrington resolved this dilemma by urging the Vietnam demonstrators to redirect their efforts toward electing a sympathetic Democrat to the presidency. In 1968, he reluctantly endorsed Hubert Humphrey in the general election, despite Humphrey's support for the war. Harrington also sharply condemned the antiwar movement for its militant tactics, which, he held, caused a polarization of public opinion and so made it more difficult to form a broad coalition to elect a Democratic administration.

This same period saw the radicalization of thousands of young people who came to the belief that the Vietnam War was a logical outcome of a system based on global intervention in support of corporate interests. Many of these new Left radicals rejected any participation in the electoral arena, but there were revolutionary socialists who were actively involved in organizing militant demonstrations and who argued the necessity for independent political action. The highpoint of this drive was reached in 1968 when radicals from several states formed independent parties, such as the California Peace and Freedom party, in order to challenge directly liberal reformism. Harrington was particularly incensed by these third-party efforts because they emphasized the gap between liberal and radical perspectives toward social change, while a realignment perspective aimed at submerging these differences within a broad progressive coalition.

At present, with the widespread demoralization of the Left, ideological debates often appear to be an irrelevant luxury. Yet periods of relative quiescence are often followed by periods of militant activism. Disagreements that have seemed academic quickly become urgent. In a period of mass action, socialists who have been working within the Democratic party frequently stand with liberal leadership groups who seek to mediate the conflict, while socialists who have remained committed to an independent politics are found alongside of the militant rank and file of social movements. This division could not be more crucial.

NOTES

1. The classic statement of the supposed correlation between plurality elections and a two-party system can be found in Maurice Duverger, *Political Parties*, 2nd ed. (New York: Wiley, 1963), p. 217.

2. This is based on data from the Historical Archives of the Inter-University Consortium for Political and Social Research. I have developed the argument further in an unpublished article, "The Electoral System and Third Parties: The Socialist Party as Case Study."

3. Seymour Martin Lipset, *Agrarian Socialism* (Berkeley: University of California Press, 1959), pp. 169–72.

4. Ira Kipnis, *The American Socialist Movement, 1897–1912* (New York: Columbia University Press, 1952), pp. 272–76.

BIBLIOGRAPHY

Addes, George. Papers. Walter P. Reuther Library, Wayne State University, Detroit, Michigan.

Reuther, Roy. Papers. Walter P. Reuther Library, Wayne State University, Detroit, Michigan.

Socialist Party. Papers. William R. Perkins Library, Duke University, Durham, North Carolina. Microfilmed as *Socialist Party of America Papers, 1897–1963*. Glen Rock, New Jersey: Microfilming Corporation of America, 1975; and as *Socialist Party of America Papers, 1919–76 Addendum*. Glen Rock, New Jersey: Microfilming Corporation of America, 1977.

Workers Party and Independent Socialist League. Papers. Collated as *Independent Socialist Mimeographia*. Berkeley, California: Independent Socialist Press, 1971.

NEWSPAPERS

The Daily Worker
Detroit Free Press
Detroit News
The Democratic Left
Labor Action
The Militant
New York Times
Pontiac Auto Worker
Socialist Appeal
Socialist Call
United Automobile Worker
Village Voice
West Side Conveyor
Workers Age

BOOKS AND JOURNALS

Barnard, John. *Walter Reuther and the Rise of the Auto Workers*. Boston: Little, Brown, 1983.

Borkenau, Franz. *The Communist International.* London: Faber and Faber, 1938.

Browder, Earl. *The Meaning of Social Fascism.* New York: Workers Library, 1933.

_____ . *What Is the New Deal?* New York: Workers Library, 1933.

_____ . *Communism in the United States.* New York: International, 1935.

_____ . "United Front—The Key to Our New Tactical Orientation." *Communist* 14 (December 1935): 1075–1129.

_____ . *What is Communism?* New York: Workers Library, 1936.

_____ . "The Results of the Elections and the Popular Front." *Communist* 16 (January 1937): 14–49.

_____ . "Communists in the Popular Front." *Communist* 16 (July 1937): 594–629.

_____ . *Concerted Action or Isolation.* New York: Workers Library, 1938.

_____ . *The Democratic Front.* New York: Workers Library, 1938.

_____ . *The People's Front.* New York: International, 1938.

_____ . *Social and National Security.* New York: Workers Library, 1938.

_____ . *The 1940 Elections.* New York: Workers Library, 1939.

_____ . "Mastery of Theory and Methods of Work." *Communist* 18 (January 1939): 17–24.

_____ . *The Most Peculiar Election.* New York: Workers Library, 1940.

_____ . *Earl Browder Says.* New York: Workers Library, 1941.

_____ . *America's Decisive Battle.* New York: New Century, 1945.

_____ . "The American Communist Party in the Thirties." In *The Thirties As We Saw It*, edited by Rita James Simon, pp. 216–53. Urbana: University of Illinois, 1967.

Buck, Tim. *Reminiscences.* Toronto: NC Press, 1977.

Burns, James McGregor. *The Lion and the Fox.* New York: Harcourt Brace, 1956.

Camejo, Peter and Harrington, Michael. *Lesser Evil? The Left Debates the Democratic Party and Social Change.* New York: Pathfinder, 1977.

Cannon, James P. *The History of American Trotskyism.* New York: Pioneer, 1944.

Cochran, Bert. *Labor and Communism.* Princeton, New Jersey: Princeton University Press, 1977.

Coletta, Paolo. *William Jennings Bryan, Political Evangelist.* Lincoln: University of Nebraska Press, 1964.

Communist Party. *An Open Letter to All Members of the Communist Party.* New York: Central Committee, 1933.

Congress of Industrial Organizations, *Proceedings of the Sixteenth Constitutional Convention.* Washington, D.C.: 1954.

Congressional Quarterly. *Guide to U.S. Elections.* Washington, D.C.: 1975.

Cormier, Frank and Eaton, William J. *Reuther.* Englewood Cliffs, New Jersey: Prentice-Hall, 1970.

Debs, Eugene V. *Writings and Speeches of Eugene V. Debs.* Edited by Arthur M. Schlesinger, Jr. New York: Hermitage, 1948.

Dennis, Eugene (Francis X. Waldron, Jr.). "Some Questions Concerning the Democratic Front." *Communist* 17 (June 1938): 534–40.

_____ . "Post-War Labor–Capital Cooperation." *Political Affairs* 24 (May 1945): 415–22.

_____ . *America at the Crossroads.* New York: New Century, 1946.

Dobbs, Farrell. *Teamster Politics.* New York: Monad, 1975.

Draper, Hal (Paul Temple). "For the Present Party Position." *New International* 4 (August 1938): 229–31.

Draper, Theodore. *The Roots of American Communism.* New York: Viking, 1957.

_____ . *American Communism and Soviet Russia.* New York: Viking, 1960.

Duram, James C. "Algernon Lee's Correspondence with Karl Kautsky." *Labor History* 20 (Summer 1979): 420–34.

Duverger, Maurice. *Political Parties*, 2nd ed. London: Methuen, 1959.

Engels, Frederick. *The British Labour Movement.* New York: International, 1940.

_____ . *The Condition of the Working Class in England.* Translated by W.O. Henderson and W.H. Chaloner. London: Basil Blackwell, 1958.

Foster, James C. *The Union Politic*. Columbia: University of Missouri Press, 1975.

Foster, William Z. *The Words and Deeds of Franklin D. Roosevelt*. New York: Workers Library, 1932.

_____. *The Crisis in the Socialist Party*. New York: Workers Library, 1936.

Fountain, Clayton. *Union Guy*. New York: Viking, 1949.

Galenson, Walter. *The CIO Challenge to the AFL*. Cambridge, Massachusetts: Harvard University Press, 1960.

Gallup, George. *The Gallup Polls, 1935-71*. New York: Random House, 1972.

Gates, John (Israel Regenstreif). *Story of an American Communist*. New York: Thomas Nelson, 1958.

Gebert, B.K. "The Convention of 400,000." *Communist* 16 (October 1937): 891–905.

Gieske, Millard. *Minnesota Farmer-Laborism: The Third Party Alternative*. Minneapolis: University of Minnesota, 1979.

Glotzer, Albert (Albert Gates). "The Case for Socialist Regroupment." *New International* 23 (Spring 1957): 71–80.

_____. "Max Shachtman—A Political-Biographical Essay." *Bulletin of the Tamiment Institute* (April 1983): 3–9.

Gordon, Max. "The Communist Party and the New Left." *Socialist Revolution* 6 (January 1976): 11–47.

Green, James R., *Grass-Roots Socialism*. Baton Rouge: Louisiana State University, Press, 1976.

Hammen, Oscar. *The Red 48ers*. New York: Charles Scribners, 1969.

Harrington, Michael. "1960 Elections Predicted." *Liberation* 5 (October 1960): 10–13.

_____. "After the Union Ball." *Commonweal* 75 (November 3, 1961): 143–45.

_____. *The Other America: Poverty in the United States*. New York: Macmillan, 1962.

_____. "Voting the Lesser Evil." *Commentary* 45 (April 1968): 22–30.

_____. "Letters." *Commentary* 46 (July 1968): 16-17.

_____. *Socialism.* New York: Saturday Review, 1972.

_____. "A Call to American Socialists." *The Nation* 215 (November 13, 1972): 454-55.

_____. *Fragments of a Century.* New York: EP Dutton, 1973.

_____. "The Socialist Party." In *History of U.S. Political Parties, From Square Deal to New Deal*, edited by Arthur M. Schlesinger, Jr., pp. 2397-2444. New York: Chelsea, 1973.

_____. "Prospects for a Peace Movement." *The Nation* 216 (June 11, 1973): 742-45.

_____. "1980 and Beyond: The DSOC and the Left." *Socialist Review* 9 (July-August 1979): 15-50.

Hathaway, Clarence. "Problems In Our Farmer-Labor Party Activities." *Communist* 15 (May 1936): 427-33.

Hofstadter, Richard. *The Age of Reform.* New York: Alfred A. Knopf, 1956.

Howe, Irving (R. Fahan). "What Makes Henry Run." *New International* 14 (February 1948): 54-57.

Howe, Irving and Widick, B.J. *The UAW and Walter Reuther.* New York: Random House, 1949.

Ignike (pseud.). "Our Tactics." *International Socialist Review* 5 (July 1904): 92-97.

Independent Labour Party. *Report of the First General Conference.* Glasgow: 1893.

Independent Socialist League. "Social Forces, Politics in the U.S." *New International* 17 (July-August 1951): 207-21.

Johnpoll, Bernard K. *Prophet's Progress.* Chicago: Quadrangle Books, 1970.

Kapp, Yvonne. *Eleanor Marx*, 2 vols. London: Lawrence and Wishart, 1972-76.

Keeran, Roger. *The Communist Party and the Auto Worker.* Bloomington, Indiana: Indiana University Press, 1980.

Kipnis, Ira. *The American Socialist Movement, 1897-1912.* New York: Columbia University Press, 1952.

Kirkpatrick, Jeanne. *Dictatorships and Double Standards.* New York: Simon and Schuster, 1982.

Klehr, Harvey. *The Heyday of American Communism.* New York: Basic Books, 1984.

Lenin, V.I. "The Presidential Election in 1912." *Communist* 7 (February 1928): 67–68.

Leuchtenburg, William E. *Franklin D. Roosevelt and the New Deal, 1932–40.* New York: Harper and Row, 1963.

MacDougall, Curtis. *Gideon's Army.* New York: Marzani and Munsell, 1965.

MacKenzie, Norman and Mackenzie, Jeanne. *The First Fabians.* London: Weidenfeld and Nicolson, 1977.

McKinney, E.R. (David Coolidge). "The UAW Convention." *New International* 7 (August 1941): 70–73.

Maney, Patrick J. *Young Bob LaFollette.* Columbia: University of Missouri Press, 1978.

Marquart, Frank. *An Auto Worker's Journal.* University Park, Pennsylvania: Pennsylvania State University Press, 1975.

Marx, Karl. "Address of the Central Committee to the Communist League." In *On Revolution* ed. Saul Padover. New York: McGraw-Hill, 1971.

————. "From a Letter to Engels." In *On America and the Civil War* ed. Saul Padover. New York: McGraw-Hill, 1972.

Marx, Karl and Engels, Frederick. *Selected Correspondence, 1846–95.* New York: International, 1940.

————. *Letters to Americans.* New York: International, 1953.

————. *On Britain.* London: Lawrence and Wishart, 1954.

————. *Werke*, vol. 38. Berlin: Dietz Verlag, 1968.

Marx, Karl, Engels, Frederick, and Lenin, V.I. *On Anarchism and Anarcho-Syndicalism.* Moscow: Progress, 1972.

Mehring, Franz. *Karl Marx.* Translated by Edward Fitzgerald. Ann Arbor: University of Michigan Press, 1962.

Minor, Robert. *The Heritage of the Communist Political Association.* New York: Workers Library, 1944.

Myers, Constance Ashton. *The Prophet's Army.* Westport, Connecticut: Greenwood, 1977.

Pease, Edward R. *The History of the Fabian Society.* London: A.C. Fifield, 1916.

Pelling, Henry. *A Short History of the Labour Party.* London: Macmillan, 1961.

———. *The Origins of the Labour Party, 1880–1900.* Oxford: Clarendon, 1965.

Poirier, Phillip P. *The Advent of the British Labour Party.* New York: Columbia University Press, 1958.

Preis, Art. *Labor's Giant Step, Twenty Years of the CIO.* New York: Pioneer, 1964.

Reuther, Victor. *The Brothers Reuther.* Boston: Houghton Mifflin, 1979.

Roosevelt, Franklin D. *Nothing to Fear, Selected Addresses.* Edited by B.D. Zevin. Cambridge, Massachusetts: Houghton Mifflin, 1946.

Ruthenberg, Charles. *Speeches and Writings.* New York: International, 1928.

Schorske, Carl. *German Social Democracy, 1905–17.* New York: Russell and Russell, 1955.

Seidler, Murray G. *Norman Thomas: The Respectable Rebel.* Syracuse, New York: Syracuse University Press, 1961.

Shachtman, Max. "The Problems of the Labor Party." *New International* 2 (March 1935): 33–37.

———. "Prospects for a Labour Party." *Socialist Appeal* 3 (February 1937): 15–16.

———. "Blitzkrieg and Revolution." *New International* 6 (May 1940): 80–86.

———. "Editor's Comments." *New International* 6 (October 1940): 179–82.

———. "Labor and Strikes in Wartime." *New International* 7 (April 1941): 38–40.

———. "Editor's Comments." *New International* 7 (August 1941): 163–67.

———. "The Miners Strike and the Labor Party." *New International* 9 (July 1943): 197–98.

_____ . "The PAC, the Elections and the Future." *New International* 10 (October 1944): 307–8.

_____ . "The PAC and the Elections." *New International* 10 (November 1944): 355–57.

_____ . "UAW vs. GM." *New International* 11 (December 1945): 259–62.

_____ . *The Bureaucratic Revolution*. New York: Donald Press, 1962.

Shachtman, Max and Burnham, James. "The Question of a Labor Party." *New International* 4 (August 1938): 227–28.

Shannon, David A. *The Socialist Party of America*. New York: Macmillan, 1955.

_____ . *The Decline of American Communism*. New York: Harcourt Brace, 1959.

(Shaw, George Bernard.) *Election Manifesto of 1892*. London: Fabian Society, 1892.

(_____ .) *Report on Fabian Policy*. London: Fabian Society, 1896.

Sigal, Clancy. *Going Away*. New York: Houghton Mifflin, 1961.

Socialist Party. *The Socialist Campaign Book of 1900*. Chicago: Charles Kerr, 1900.

_____ . *National Convention of the Socialist Party*. Chicago: 1904.

_____ . *National Convention of the Socialist Party*. Chicago: 1912.

Stachel, Jack. "Build the Party for Peace, Democracy and Socialism." *Communist* 17 (March 1938): 220–41.

Starobin, Joseph R. *American Communism in Crisis, 1943–57*. Cambridge, Massachusetts: Harvard University Press, 1972.

Trotsky, Leon. *The Transitional Program for a Socialist Revolution*. New York: Pathfinder, 1973.

_____ . "The Labor Party Question." In *Writings of Leon Trotsky*, 1932 ed. George Breitman and Sarah Lovell. New York: Pathfinder, 1973.

_____ . "Discussions with Max Shachtman." In *Writings of Leon Trotsky, Supplement 1929–33* ed. George Breitman and Sarah Lovell. New York: Pathfinder, 1979.

United Automobile Workers of America. *Proceedings of the Second Annual Convention*. Detroit: 1936.

―――. *Proceedings of the Third Annual Convention*. Detroit: 1936.

U.S. Bureau of the Census. *Historical Statistics of the United States*, 2 vols. Washington, D.C.: GPO 1975.

U.S. Senate. Committee on Foreign Relations. *Recognition of Russia*, 68th Cong., 2nd Sess., 1924. Washington, D.C.: 1924.

Ward's Communications. *Ward's Automotive Year Book*. Detroit: 1938.

Ward's Communications. *Ward's Automotive Year Book*. Detroit: 1943.

Weinstein, James. *The Decline of Socialism in America, 1912-25*. New York: Monthly Review, 1967.

Weinstone, William (William Winestein). "The Great Auto Strike." *Communist* 16 (March 1937): 201-28.

Whitaker, Joseph. *Whitaker's Almanac*. London: 1896.

Winston, Henry. "Towards a Party of 100,000." *Political Affairs* 26 (January 1947): 64-79.

―――. "For a Fighting Party Rooted Among the Industrial Workers." *Political Affairs* 27 (September 1948): 834-56.

Workers Party. "The Fight for a Labor Party." *New International* 9 (December 1943): 329-31.

INDEX

Abner, Willoughby, 119–20
Addes, George, 108–10, 113, 114–15.
    See also UAW
AFL, 67
AFL-CIO, 134–35, 142–43, 145
Americans for Democratic Action
    (ADA), 131
Automobile Workers Union (AWU), 67

Benson, Herman, 111–12, 115, 118,
    120–22, 123, 125–26. *See also* In-
    dependent Socialist League;
    Workers Party
Berger, Victor, 32, 33, 35
Bieber, Owen, 144
Bloc voting, 27, 102
Browder, Earl: and Catholic Church,
    45–6; and Democratic party,
    44–5; and independent political
    action, 43, 45; and John L.
    Lewis, 69; and Homer Martin,
    85; on New Deal, 55–6; on
    patriotism, 45; and Pontiac
    strike, 82, and post-war period,
    47; on Franklin Roosevelt, 43,
    46, 53–6; on Socialist party, 43,
    51; on strikes, 73–74. *See also*
    Communist Party
Bryan, William Jennings, 31
Burnham, James, 101–02

Cannon James P., 95, 100. *See also*
    Trotskyists
Catholic Church, 45–46
Chrysler Corporation, 70–71
CIO, 65–66, 69–70, 86, 100. *See also*
    UAW
Communist International (Comintern),
    67
Communist League, 13–4

Communist League of America (CLA),
    96–97
Communist Party (USA); and Auto
    Workers Union, 67; and Catholic
    Church, 45–46; and CIO, 65, 69,
    70; and Democratic party, 44–5,
    56–57; and Flint sit-down, 69;
    formation of, 41–42; Michael
    Harrington on, 51; and labor
    party, 42, 43–44, 45, 46, 59; and
    Ludlow Amendment, 83–84;
    membership in, 58–59; and New
    Deal, 43, 45, 55–57, 156–57; in
    1956, 123; and 1936 election, 44;
    and Pontiac strike, 79–80, 81–83;
    realignment, 45, 156; and Walter
    Reuther, 77–78, 86; and Franklin
    Roosevelt, 46, 52–57; and So-
    cialist party, 77; and Trotskyists,
    95–97; and UAW, 68, 73–76, 81,
    83–86; and Henry Wallace,
    47–48, 115; and World War II,
    46–7; and Workers party, 108–9,
    115, 116–17, 123
Communist Political Association, 46
Cooperative Commonwealth Federa-
    tion (CCF), 5, 155

Debs Caucus, 140, 142, 143. *See also*
    Socialist party
Debs, Eugene Victor, 31, 32, 33–34,
    154
Democratic Agenda, 143, 145
Democratic Front, 56
Democratic Party: and CIO, 111–12; as
    coalition, 7–8; and Communist
    party, 42, 44, 47, 54–55; and
    Democratic Socialists of
    America, 143, 145–46; Harr-
    ington on, 133, 138–39, 142, 145;

168

ABOUT THE AUTHOR

ERIC THOMAS CHESTER was Assistant Professor of Economics at the University of Massachusetts in Boston and then Lecturer at San Francisco State University in 1980. In the 1960s, Dr. Chester was active in the civil rights movement and in Students for a Democratic Society. He is currently a cab driver, an antimilitarist activist, and a member of the Socialist party.

Dr. Chester has published widely in the areas of economics, labor history, and political sociology. His articles have appeared in the *Cambridge Journal of Economics, Insurgent Sociologist, Public Finance, Against the Current,* and *Changes.*

Dr. Chester holds a B.A. and a Ph.D. from the University of Michigan in Ann Arbor.

Université d'Otta.

E. . . . .